Twayne's United States Authors Series

EDITOR OF THIS VOLUME

Warren French

Indiana University

Shirley Ann Grau

TUSAS 382

Photograph © 1977 by Jill Krementz

Shirley Ann Grau

SHIRLEY ANN GRAU

By Paul Schlueter

TWAYNE PUBLISHERS
A DIVISION OF G. K. HALL & CO., BOSTON

Published in 1981 by Twayne Publishers,
A Division of G. K. Hall & Co.
All Rights Reserved

Printed on permanent/durable acid-free paper and bound
in the United States of America

First Printing

Frontispiece photo of Shirley Ann Grau © by Jill Krementz

Library of Congress Cataloging in Publication Data

Schlueter, Paul, 1933–
Shirley Ann Grau.

(Twayne's United States authors series ; TUSAS 382)
Bibliography: p. 150–55
Includes index.
1. Grau, Shirley Ann—Criticism and interpretation.
PS3557.R283Z86   813'.54   80-29122
ISBN 0-8057-7316-9

Contents

About the Author

Paul Schlueter received degrees in English from the University of Minnesota and the University of Denver and his Ph.D. in English from Southern Illinois University. He has taught at several American colleges and universities and served as guest professor at three German universities. He has published essays, reviews, and bibliographies on a wide range of subjects, including Mary McCarthy, Richard Aldington, Doris Lessing, religion and literature, Canadian literature, and Albert Camus, with his book *The Novels of Doris Lessing* (Southern Illinois University Press, 1973) the first major critical study of this author. He edited Lessing's essays (*A Small Personal Voice: Essays, Reviews, and Interviews* [Knopf, 1974]), as well as collections of essays on Lessing, Thornton Wilder, "The Sacred and the Obscene," and "The Administration of Research," and contributed to the *Encyclopaedia Britannica* and the *Encyclopedia of World Literature in the Twentieth Century*. Former editor of *Christianity and Literature*, he has held several offices in the Indiana College English Association and the Conference on Christianity and Literature, he served for several years on the Executive Committee of the Religious Approaches to Literature Division of the Modern Language Association, and he planned and directed literary conferences, including a Bicentennial conference on New Jersey's Literary Heritage. At present he is doing research for several other book projects and writing free-lance criticism and essays from his home in Easton, Pennsylvania.

Preface

Shirley Ann Grau has been an established writer of fiction for some thirty years, and in that time she has received both critical and popular acclaim, though less critical attention than a writer of her ability deserves. Hence a book-length study of her entire literary output (aside from uncollected short stories and nonfiction periodical writing such as reviews) seems both appropriate and timely. Oddly, though, a good deal of the coverage of her work, such as newspaper and magazine reviews, has been so uncomprehending as to reflect more hostility than analysis, and she has suffered such pejorative and patronizing categorization as a mere "writing housewife," a producer of "southern gothic" or "local-color" novels, and an author more appropriate for women's magazines and clubs than for scholarship. Such terms are typical of the misunderstanding that some of her work has prompted, and while she is hardly free from faults as a writer, a sustained study has long been needed to show the relationship among her individual works, to demonstrate how her strong sense of locale and convictions about forces such as power and love operate in her characters' lives, and to delineate those aspects of her fiction that warrant even further analysis.

To be sure, she cannot be considered a major southern writer, nor as a preeminent spokesman for any uniquely "southern" point of view on controversial matters; yet her sense of "place" so dominates her work that no analysis can ignore this aspect of her writing. Her shortcomings as a creator of well-structured plots (often mentioned in critiques) and her tendency to create some major characters who lack emotional depth are valid observations, but so are the comments that many of her characters are among the most memorable in recent American fiction. And her stylistic excellence—her ability, for example, to create vivid sensory images that echo in the reader's mind long after the work is finished—is also notable, even though her ability to develop and use symbolic language sometimes falters. In short, she is a talented but inconsistent writer, and this study attempts to show how both extremes, sometimes even in the same book, reflect the impossibility of dismissing her as a writer with nothing to say to a reader interested in literary excellence.

Grau's first book, *The Black Prince and Other Stories* (1955), was an inordinately praised collection that led to many comparisons with the work of McCullers, O'Connor, and Welty. Grau's accomplishments in this collection and in one later selection, *The Wind Shifting West* (1973), are mixed and inconsistent; despite those stories that can stand with the best of the short fiction of these other authors, there are a number, especially in the later collection, that simply do not succeed, thus suggesting that her ultimate place in literary history may be more as the author of two or three excellent, major novels than as a sustained practitioner of the shorter form, and so these two collections are discussed together in a final chapter of this study.

The novels, beginning with *The Hard Blue Sky* (1958), are a considerably more ambitious undertaking, and these receive the bulk of the evaluation in this study. Her first novel is a detailed, atmospherically oppressive account of primitive Cajun fishermen living on various isolated Mississippi delta islands south of New Orleans, the area serving as the setting for much of Grau's fiction. The oppressiveness of the weather, which the reader is never allowed to ignore for very long, governs and parallels the actions of the principal characters, as they fish, make love, burn down houses of those they dislike, try to escape to a more favorable locale, die, or simply survive, indomitably and stoically, whatever nature brings them. People of strong appetites and convictions, they value uniformly all that occurs between birth and death as inevitable and natural, and thus they are rarely surprised at what life brings them; instead, they simply continue. The acclaim Grau received for this novel was, in retrospect, excessive and simply impossible for most writers to surpass with their subsequent books, and Grau, too, suffered when some of her later works were compared, unfavorably, with this one.

Her second book, in fact, was a considerably lesser accomplishment than her first, and *The House on Coliseum Street* (1961) seems now to be more a study of a neurotic young woman than a successful account of the tensions created when several women, a mother and her daughters, experience various forms of lovelessness and alienation. It is less excellent than Grau's first novel, and considerably less so than her third, *The Keepers of the House* (1964), which won the Pulitzer Prize for fiction.

The Keepers of the House is a remarkable book, better than anything else Grau has done, with its excellences being many: her skillful account of the several generations in a southern dynasty (calling Faulkner to mind for many reviewers), the tensions caused by revelation of a racially mixed marriage between the patriarch in the dynasty and his housekeeper, and the dramatic closing chapters when the vigorous granddaughter of the patriarch takes on, and defeats, the entire area (including her estranged husband) in her desire to "keep" the "house" safe from destruction. Grau's handling of plot, character, setting, and underlying symbolic texture are superbly realized, and this, her most ambitious work, fully warrants both the acclaim it received upon publication and the extensive analysis provided in this study, for, like the patriarch himself, it speaks with the moral fervor and outrage of an Old Testament prophet.

The Condor Passes (1971) is also about a patriarch, but a far less exalted and heroic one. In this case, the man is an aged self-made millionaire whose fortunes have come from various illicit enterprises (bootlegging, gambling, etc.), but whose personal emotional fortunes are far from great. His daughters are an ascetic masochist and a nymphomaniacal extrovert, and since neither has any offspring who can carry on the family activities, the lineage will cease, even though the patriarch's lack of perception in human affairs is well demonstrated by his choice of a son-in-law who turns out so totally amoral as to appear subhuman. An extremely depressing book in places, this does support Grau's attempt to study those individuals with immense amounts of money who simply have impoverished emotional lives. The interplay of power and love, in fact, remains a fascinating and potentially more complicated relationship than it receives in Grau's hands, especially in her difficulties with the symbol of the condor used throughout the book.

Power and love are also the focus of *Evidence of Love* (1977), Grau's one novel set almost completely outside the South. Again concerned with an aging, successful man of business, this novel attempts to show the radical contrasts between those who, like the patriarch, cannot reflect any genuine "evidence of love," and those who, like his daughter-in-law, can handle such love, in all its various manifestations, maturely and well. In this novel Grau also explores the implications of religious faith, with the elder man's clergyman son a sharp contrast both to his father and to his own sons, who, again, seem incapable of mature love. A very successful novel, this work suggests that Grau's talents are not limited to parochial southern settings, characters, or interests, and that her fascination with the interplay of power and love both transcends regionalism and is at the heart of all of her fiction.

The hyperbolic acclaim she has received, therefore, has been offered for the wrong reasons, just as the calumny she has been accorded is excessive and serves to diminish her accomplishments, again for the wrong reasons. For, despite her limitations, she is consistently craftsmanlike in characterization, style, and setting, she is able to probe into "primitive" and powerful alike in such a way as to suggest their common abuse of and lack of understanding of power, and she can effectively create worlds in which primordial forces are in conflict. Again, the twin emphases of love and power come into her work repeatedly, with the problem of evil implied in both emphases serving as her special concern. Only rarely, however, do her characters become as complex as the reader would like, and rarely do they achieve tragic stature, even though their worlds are replete with forms of conflict, frequently violent, in which such stature could result. At her best, she has produced a number of excellent short stories and three memorable novels; but all of her writing warrants the kind of interest that would lead a reader to reexperience the work two or even more times, simply because the texture of conflict and setting are so well done.

This study, then, is an attempt to elaborate on these brief observations, to offer sustained analyses of Grau's published work, and to suggest patterns in her work for others to pursue. For there is no doubt in my mind that at her best Grau is a writer likely to be read for many years into the future, and therefore this first detailed study of her fiction is as much a recommendation as it is an analysis.

PAUL SCHLUETER

Easton, Pennsylvania

Acknowledgments

Writing a critical study such as this could not have been done without the assistance and advice of numerous friends and correspondents, for even though the body of material published on Shirley Ann Grau is not great, the efforts of those producing this material have all proved valuable. The bibliographic tasks undertaken by two scholars have been especially indispensable. Margaret S. Grissom put together the first checklist of Grau's published work, and Joseph A. Grau (no relation to Shirley Ann Grau) has built upon and expanded Grissom's bibliography by locating virtually every item published by Grau, as well as almost all the reviews, articles, and references, no matter how obscure, that relate to her work. I am deeply indebted to them for their efforts, as well as for the extensive correspondence we have shared over the years.

In addition, the library personnel at Tulane University and the *New Orleans Times-Picayune* were of great assistance in helping me locate material by or about Grau; again, I am grateful for their help.

Alfred A. Knopf, publishers of all of Grau's books, have also been of assistance, and I thank them for permitting the use of selected quotations. Sylvia Bowman, longtime editor for the TUSAS series, and her assistant, Alberta M. Hines, have been consistently encouraging in awaiting the completion of this book, and although they are no longer involved in the active editing of the series, this study could not have been written had they not been as understanding as they were.

But the greatest degree of thanks must go to Shirley Ann Grau herself, not only for many exchanges of correspondence in which we discussed matters related to her work, but even more for her candid comments in two extensive tape-recorded interviews, conducted when she graciously allowed me to visit her homes in Metairie, Louisiana, and on Martha's Vineyard, Massachusetts. Though she cannot be held responsible for my comments (and indeed may well wish to dissociate herself from some of my less favorable conclusions), she has at all times been a cooperative, helpful subject for a critical study.

Finally, I am grateful to my wife, June, to whom the book is dedicated, for her consistently sound editorial advice.

Chronology

1929 Shirley Ann Grau born July 9 in New Orleans.

1940– Attends Booth School, now-defunct girls' finishing school, in
1945 Montgomery, Alabama.

1945– Attends, and is graduated from, Ursuline Academy, Roman
1946 Catholic high school in New Orleans.

1946– Attends Sophie Newcomb College, Tulane University's college
1950 for women, in New Orleans. Studies writing under Dr. John
Husband. Several stories appear in *Carnival*, Newcomb College's undergraduate literary magazine, and one in *Surf*, a New
Orleans literary magazine.

1949 Wins annual Virginia Gleaves Lazarus Memorial Medal for best
essay by a Newcomb College junior or senior; the essay, on
Joyce and entitled "Two Portraits of the Artist," is published in
Carnival.

1950 Chosen for Phi Beta Kappa. Senior honors thesis on "John
Donne's Sermons: A Study in Style." Graduates from Newcomb
College.

1950– Begins graduate studies (primarily in Renaissance and meta-
1951 physical poetry) at Tulane University; does not finish her
degree.

1953 First professional stories published: "The Sound of Silver" and
"White Girl, Fine Girl."

1954 First story in the *New Yorker:* "Joshua." *The Black Prince and
Other Stories*.

1955 Marries James Kern Feibleman, professor of philosophy at
Tulane University. Two more stories in the *New Yorker* and
two essays in *Holiday*.

1956 Story in *New World Writing;* essay in *Holiday*.

1957 Son, Ian James, born. Story in *Mademoiselle*.

1958 *The Hard Blue Sky*, a novel; essay in *Holiday*.

1960 Daughter, Nora Miranda, born. Stories in the *Saturday Evening Post* and the *Atlantic*.

1961 *The House on Coliseum Street*, a novel; stories in *The
Reporter, Shenandoah, Story*, and the *Saturday Evening Post*.

"Foreword" to G. W. Cable, *Old Creole Days*. Both parents die.

1962 Stories in the *Atlantic*, the *Saturday Evening Post, Redbook*, and *Vogue*.

1964 Son, William, born. *The Keepers of the House*, a novel; condensed in *Ladies' Home Journal*.

1965 Wins Pulitzer Prize for fiction. Story in *Redbook*; essay in *New York Times Magazine*. Appointed by President Lyndon Johnson to Commission on Presidential Scholars.

1966 Stories in *Gentleman's Quarterly* and *Cosmopolitan*; "Introduction" to Marjorie Kinnan Rawlings, *Cross Creek*.

1966– Teaches creative writing at the University of New Orleans.
1967

1967 Daughter, Katherine, born. Stories in the *Atlantic* and the *Southern Review*.

1968 Essay in *McCall's*; stories in *Redbook* and the *Saturday Evening Post*.

1971 *The Condor Passes*, a novel.

1973 *The Wind Shifting West* (stories).

1977 *Evidence of Love*, a novel.

CHAPTER 1

"A Certain Facility with Words"

I Grau's Life and Career

WHEN the author whose work was selected as the winner of the 1965 Pulitzer Prize for fiction was called at her home with the news, she replied, "Don't be silly!" and, "This must be a practical joke!"[1] Indeed, until a telegram with the news arrived later the same day from Dr. Grayson Kirk, then president of Columbia University and administrator of the Pulitzer Prizes, she steadfastly refused to believe the news, even going so far as to call personally her publisher, Alfred A. Knopf, to ask if it were true; he in turn haughtily replied, "Yes, it's true. You won it. It's no Nobel Prize, but I guess it will have to do for the time being."[2] Indeed, it was not until later that she was aware that the prize also carried a cash award of five hundred dollars, money she subsequently used for an IBM electric typewriter.

But it was no joke: at the age of thirty-five, Shirley Ann Grau had received one of the nation's top honors for writing. One of only fifteen women till that time to have won the Pulitzer Prize, and the youngest up to that date, Grau followed a tradition extending back to Edith Wharton, first woman to be so honored, and including Willa Cather, Ellen Glasgow, Pearl Buck, and Katherine Anne Porter. Grau specifically received the award for her third novel, *The Keepers of the House*, published in April 1964 by Alfred A. Knopf, the distinguished firm that has also published all of Grau's other books as well: *The Black Prince and Other Stories* (1954); *The Hard Blue Sky*, a novel (1958); *The House on Coliseum Street*, a novel (1961); *The Condor Passes*, a novel (1971); *The Wind Shifting West*, a collection of stories (1973); and *Evidence of Love*, a novel (1977). She has in addition published a number of other short stories that are still uncollected, in virtually every major market for short fiction in this country, as well as numerous articles and book reviews.

Grau's startled reaction at being notified that she had won the Pulitzer Prize for fiction, then, may seem, in light of her productivity even before the year of the award, to be merely conventional disbelief and false modesty, particularly so in a day when writers sometimes campaign actively and tactlessly for such awards while at the same time disparaging the value of such prizes—until, that is, they happen to be the recipients, at which time they evince total and utter surprise. Grau's case, however, is slightly different, for her career, beginning with fairly typical undergraduate efforts and proceeding through years of apprenticeship work before hitting her mature stride, was a career more dedicated to the disciplined craft of fiction than to seeking awards.

Shirley Ann Grau was born in New Orleans on July 9, 1929, one of two daughters—her sister's name is Jean—born to Dr. Adolph E. Grau, a dentist, and Katherine (Onions) Grau, both of whom died in 1961. Of mixed German Lutheran, Scottish Presbyterian, and Louisiana Creole (French-Spanish) background, she had a paternal grandfather who disapproved of militarism and who left Prussia in the middle nineteenth century in time for the Civil War; she also had a maternal grandfather of the "classic" American mixture of English, Scotch, and Irish who came from a family of farmers and riverboat men; her maternal ancestors were in North Carolina in the 1740s and in Virginia in the 1720s, and another branch of the family was in Massachusetts and Rhode Island a couple of generations earlier. Hence she combines two distinct traditions—New England and Southern—but, since she never found her family very interesting, she has never maintained much interest in her heritage.[3] Her own family, she says,

wasn't poor by any means, but I don't suppose we were really rich. Nevertheless, there must have been some source of money, because nobody actually worked. Everyone seemed to have a rather cavalier attitude about money. My grandfather quit work when he was forty. He figured he had enough to live on. He was an engineer, rather a gadgeteer. He tinkered with things, useful trinkets and such. Maybe he patented something, I don't know. He must have done well. I don't know, that is, I can't be sure where it came from, the money, probably from wise stock market action, but it never occurred to me to ask. I was never bothered, because there was a big age gap. My mother was forty-five when I was born. . . . And Dad must have been fifty-five![4]

As a child, Shirley Ann and her family shuttled between New Orleans (which her mother favored) and Montgomery, Alabama (where her father preferred to live). In Montgomery she attended Booth

School, a now-defunct girls' finishing school. "It was a very solid nine-teenth-century school, with no extra-curricular activities," she says, "run by two maiden ladies named, so help me, Booth. There was some science, a lot of math, literature, and languages. As far as I remember, that was all. It was probably a very good school because, to this day, I have a good working knowledge of classical Latin."[5] She adds: "School was from 9 until 1; then everyone dashed out. It was unaccredited. They started French very early, and Latin in fourth or fifth grade. They also started Greek early; it was a typical nineteenth-century classical education. But my parents knew I had to go to college, so I had to go to an accredited high school. So we moved back to New Orleans when I was a senior and I went to Ursuline Academy for one year. Booth was a full twelve-year school, and I went there for six years. We lived in Montgomery during the war, and moved back to New Orleans just so I could finish high school at an accredited school."[6]

Ursuline, a Roman Catholic institution, was chosen by the Graus because it was the only boarding school available for Shirley and because it was the only high school in New Orleans offering Greek in addition to the Latin that Grau had been studying since fifth grade. "If you go to that sort of place and can keep your sense of humor, it's very nice. It struck me as some sort of play, with endless ritual, all those funny black figures running around; it was a very conservative order."[7] Her mother, she notes, was a Presbyterian and her father a Lutheran. As a child, she attended a Baptist Sunday School, and her grandmother sent her to the Episcopalian church. She is "officially" Baptist and Methodist, but belongs to the Unitarian church: "Unitarians are the least objectionable. The Unitarian church is where you go when you don't want to be anything."[8]

During this final year of high school, her father was in the army, away from the family, because, even though he was in his seventies at the time, surgeons experienced in facial reconstruction were urgently needed. She tried to get into Tulane University, but at that time women were allowed only into Tulane's women's division, Sophie Newcomb College, which she labels as a "kind of finishing school," and where the students tried persistently to get into classes with Tulane men. She says now that she recalls both Ursuline and Booth well, but that her college years at Newcomb are a blur. She attended Newcomb from 1946 to 1950, graduating with honors in English. But Newcomb, she says, was far from all peace and tranquillity. "I found athletics and sororities a bore. As a matter of fact, they threatened to throw me out

of Newcomb for failing all my gym classes. I didn't go, because I didn't
want to be a flower in modern dance. I did go to swimming, and that
was great. But shooting arrows—I didn't want any of that. But they
wouldn't throw anyone out with a decent academic record."[9] She did
participate in two extracurricular activities, according to records at
Tulane for the years in question: International Relations Club and the
German Club. She was, in fact, president of the German Club in
1949–1950, and she was elected to Phi Beta Kappa the same year. In
her last year at Newcomb she also served as associate editor of *Carnival*, the campus literary quarterly, and for two years following her
graduation she was graduate editor.

Her feelings about Newcomb are somewhat reflected in this observation: "If you're a scholar teaching at Newcomb, you know you'll
never produce a scholar—only mothers."[10] But, she adds, "one nice
thing about a college in a city is that you're not dependent on it. And
if you find yourself at a school like Newcomb, this is all to the good.
New Orleans is a wonderful and exciting city for an 18-year-old girl."[11]
Since Newcomb did not allow its nonresident students to live off-cam-
pus, unless living with family, she officially lived with her parents; during her senior year and one year afterward she lived in an apartment
overlooking a huge courtyard in the French Quarter, at 921 Chartres
Street, with a close friend, Mary Rohrberger, then a social worker in
New Orleans and now professor of English at Oklahoma State University, Stillwater. "When you're eighteen you don't notice that the
French Quarter is so tawdry. . . . The Quarter in those days was very
quiet, not touristy, and we all knew each other," Grau says. "There
were a lot of beginning writers and musicians and bright people just
out of college living there."[12] Among those graduating from Tulane
with Grau in 1950, for example, was the noted journalist Tom Wicker
of the *New York Times*.

Even though Grau, like many writers, had made youthful efforts at
creating imaginary worlds and characters through words, it was not
until her Newcomb experience that she began in earnest by studying
writing under Professor John Husband, who encouraged her work as
it developed into something more mature than the usual undergraduate writing. Dr. Husband is justifiably proud of his student, and he has
said, "I taught her for three years. . . . When Shirley Ann first came to
my classes I didn't sense any special talent. She was a systematic
worker; she was intelligent. She told me then that she had made up her
mind to be a writer and wanted to do all the work that was necessary
and learn all that was necessary to achieve this goal."[13] Grau wrote a

number of stories for Dr. Husband's class, several of which were subsequently published in *Carnival;* she also had several poems published in that magazine. And she had one story published in *Surf,* a New Orleans literary magazine published by J. Buchanan Blitch, a prominent architect in the city. One story written for Dr. Husband's class, entitled by him "The Silver Penny," was subsequently revised and published as "The Sound of Silver" in the *New Mexico Quarterly* in 1953, three years after Grau's graduation from college; this, her first professionally published piece, earned her the grand sum of twenty-five dollars. (This story was subsequently republished—with Grau's original title—as the title story in her first book, the collection *The Black Prince and Other Stories* [1954].)

Another of the stories written for *Carnival,* "The Fragile Age," was singled out in a section of the magazine entitled "Our Campus Critics Respond," with such terms as "highly original in conception and treatment," "subtle wit seldom encountered in today's literature," and "forceful in its technical mastery of dramatic underplaying, its carefully selected diction, its quick pace of action," along with a few less complimentary comments.[14] An essay by Grau on James Joyce, "Two Portraits of the Artist,"[15] won the 1949 Virginia Gleaves Lazarus Memorial Medal for the best essay written by a Newcomb junior or senior. Grau's piece is typical undergraduate criticism in its facile judgments, yet it does demonstrate an articulate handling of diction and structure with an ability to probe into the work's meaning. Chosen for membership by Phi Beta Kappa during her senior year, she wrote her twenty-nine-page honors thesis on "John Donne's Sermons: A Study in Style," demonstrating an awareness of rhetoric in Donne's writing subsequently practiced in her own style.

Grau's father had told her that he would not support her in graduate school unless she were "doing something," which he did not believe was true of writing. Nonetheless, she began study for her master's degree (never completed) at Tulane the year she graduated, 1950, a year she calls "merely a filler-in year" in which she took course work in English, primarily in Renaissance and metaphysical poetry, and continued writing during and after that year. The sale of "The Sound of Silver" to the *New Mexico Quarterly* in 1953 was a major step toward proving that she could sell her writing; in the same year she sold "White Girl, Fine Girl" to *New World Writing,* Fourth Mentor Selection, for which she received two payments, of $250 and $95;[16] then "Joshua" was sold to the *New Yorker* for "considerably more."[17] And when *The Black Prince and Other Stories* appeared in 1954, the first printing was sold out in two weeks' time.[18] Needless to say, Grau's father was by this time persuaded that writing was not only a possible career for his daughter but a profitable one as well. Since the contacts for writers were primarily in New York, Grau now considered moving there while simultaneously continuing to keep her Chartres Street apartment. Instead, she stayed in New Orleans and continued to write until her marriage the following year, 1955.

She had already long since given up an early career plan to become a lawyer, because, she said, "one might as well be practical. No woman [then had] very much of a chance in law—she [had] to fight too hard."[19] Writing, though, was an option because "there was no prejudice against women. In fact, being a woman has a slight advantage, especially in nonfiction. Not much, but a little. And second, writing required no organization. The regular sort of job I wouldn't do, the kind with everything so organized. So, you see, I guess I became a writer by the process of elimination. I certainly never became a writer as a matter of compensation for something, like so many others say they have. I just don't fit in that category, the one where authors complain about their unhappy childhoods and about being so socially alienated."[20]

On August 4, 1955, Grau, then twenty-five, married James Kern Feibleman, then fifty-one, and, until his recent retirement, chairman of the Tulane University philosophy department. Feibleman is an example of the modern Renaissance man: he is self-educated, with but two months of college to his name, but he has written some thirty books thus far, covering such topics and subject areas as philosophy, psychiatry, education, government, aesthetics, literary criticism, drama, poetry, fiction, sociology, and others. His autobiography, *The Way of a Man*, was published in 1969, and demonstrates quite thoroughly his interests in all of contemporary life, surely far more than is true of any comparable figure in American philosophy, as well as his personal acquaintances with many of the century's major writers and thinkers, including Faulkner, Sherwood Anderson, and Einstein. Feibleman is the father, from a previous marriage, of Peter Feibleman, young author whose first novel, *A Place Without Twilight*, was published in 1958, and who has published other novels, a cookbook (on Spain and Portugal), screenplays, and a successfully produced Broadway play in the years since. Born in 1930, he is one year younger than his stepmother. Shirley Ann and James Feibleman have four children: Ian James, born in 1957; Nora Miranda, born in 1960; William, born in 1964; and Katherine, born in 1967; all are named after their grandparents. The Feiblemans live in the New Orleans suburb of Metairie, in a spacious residence Feibleman had built in 1938, following a design by Walter Gropius, and subsequently sold and repurchased for his current family.

Summers are spent by the Feiblemans in a rambling old farmhouse that they rented sight unseen for their honeymoon and bought the year after, at Chilmark, on Martha's Vineyard, Massachusetts, where the family also goes at other times of the year. Martha's Vineyard, which swells some tenfold in population each summer to 50,000 or more, and where summer homes are priced out of the market for all but the most affluent, had long been a popular retreat for writers, artists, scholars, businessmen, and others; Grau's praise for the Vineyard resulted in a 1965 article entitled "The Vineyard Is 'The Place To Go'"[21] in which she recounts a number of anecdotes about the inexplicable but certain appeal of the place.

Both the Chilmark and Metairie residences, Grau says, are "noisy, crowded, filled with people rushing off to do something. . . . But we manage. Somehow we always do. And somehow I always find the time I need for my work." Her life, she says, is a "conventional upper middle-class life. My husband is a businessman (for a living) and a professor of philosophy (for love of the field)." Some years back she commented that she loves to swim, and that her hobbies include modern sculpture and painting, folksongs, and reading history, biography, and travel books. She also enjoys tennis, plays the violin (badly, she says), and enjoys fishing and sailing. She loves the steamy heat of the tropics and subtropics and hates the cold.

Now a mother of four children, Shirley Ann Grau is successful as both a family person and a writer. She has had two collections of short stories and five novels published, as well as many uncollected stories, magazine articles, and book reviews. Still in her fifties, Grau is likely to continue to produce some of the richest writing being produced in the South since the writers one often thinks of as uniquely "Southern"—Faulkner, Welty, O'Connor, McCullers, others—were in their prime.

II Grau as a "Southern" Writer

It is easy, too easy, to categorize Grau as a "Southern" writer by virtue of the fact that she has lived in Louisiana and Alabama all her life, as well as the fact that most of her fiction is set in the Gulf states. She has been included in anthologies of Southern writing, and she has been discussed critically as a "Southern" writer.[22] But the south is no more homogeneous and monolithic than is the American midwest; characteristics of a writer in Texas differ considerably from those in, say, Florida—and yet both, along with all the geographic gradations in between, are loosely labeled "Southern." Grau has commented that "it's unfortunate that every novel laid in the South is labeled as a 'Southern Novel.' "[23] In most cases, this labeling occurs because of subject matter such as the relations between whites and blacks, but even this is not sufficient to serve as an adequate explanation for the facile way in which a regional novelist such as Grau is grouped with every other writer from her region as if this were tantamount to a critical judgment.

Grau, when asked whether she considers herself as part of any Southern literary tradition, commented, "I hope not!" and then added that she could not then (1969) think of a single Southern writer whom she admired. She did not care for Faulkner, whom her husband knew well, finding Faulkner's "conception rather cheap, though perhaps it was good in the 1930s." Grau believes that Eudora Welty was "very skillful for her day, but she's spun herself so thin that she's almost transparent." Carson McCullers "had a lot of strength, a lot more thought in her," compared to Welty. But Flannery O'Connor "went the other way; she spun herself in knots. She took the wrong turn, probably because of those heavy religious kicks she went on. You can get so turned around in your gothic trappings that you lose sight of where you are. I suppose I admire Carson McCullers the most; for as bad as her execution was at times, at least she had an idea." She finds Welty lacking in compassion for her characters, even though, she says, "if you were going to teach short-story writing, I don't know of anyone whom you could teach any better than Welty. She constructs divinely!"[24]

The South itself, Grau comments, is a "wonderful place to live" in, one section of the country where "things have improved . . . enormously":

You don't see those little one-mule farms any more, kids with wormy bellies, the nasty backlash of poverty that used to glare at you. The towns look so prosperous, it makes for a cheery atmosphere, a sense of everything improving.

I like the South and I dislike it. You find yourself swinging back and forth madly. After a racial incident, I'm furious. People say, "Why don't you leave the south?" And I say, "I'd just as soon stay here. I can see the improvement."[25]

These comments, however, should not lead one to conclude that Grau takes a Pollyanna-like stance regarding evil found in mankind, nor that she is concerned with writing ameliorative tracts about Southern progress; it is, rather, that she can see the changes that have taken place over the past thirty years, notably in regard to racial tensions.

Grau has commented that "race is the only issue in the South, really. The pressure has forced people to one side or the other. And the poor old South, it is exactly like someone's poor relation. It is so touchy, so easily insulted, so infuriating."[26] She considers herself as a "moderate" between the extremes, liking neither busing nor violence, even though she finds it increasingly difficult to maintain the middle ground where she tries to be. She comments, "I think the South got itself into the mess it's in, so now it's all coming back home."

Ironically, she has been criticized for giving a "too-sympathetic" portrayal of both blacks and whites in her novels, and each race has been annoyed by favorable characterizations of the other, notably in *The Keepers of the House*. Following the publication of that novel in 1964, some white Southerners called her a traitor to the South for her picture of Southern blacks, leading, among other things, to abusive late-night phone calls, cessation of friendships with segregationist acquaintances, and a reaction from her own family of feeling "rather miffed." Similarly, the Southern white male, she felt, was often unjustly libeled as running around the countryside roads with a white sheet and shotgun. Some of Grau's "liberal" friends told her there was no such thing as a "good southern white," which she considers "ridiculous; he can be a very fine human being."[27]

Blacks, on the other hand, objected that a Negro woman in *The Keepers of the House* was too bewitched by a white man in the novel, to which Grau responds, "But I was raised by that kind of woman. I've seen their houses and their swept dirt yards. I've known some who knocked themselves out to get their children north. I've seen the tremendously strong attraction between black and white, the violent feelings they have for each other, love as well as hate."[28]

In 1966 Grau was quoted as believing that only "sheer exhaustion" will ever make the South ease its fight against integration;[29] the years since have surely led to a state of rapprochement that makes even her earlier controversial work seem muted by comparison with today's less-controversial fictional accounts of racial contact. Even *The Keepers of the House*, as explicitly about race as it was, was not so much about segregation, Grau believes, as is work by James Baldwin.

Segregation and the entire "Southern obsession" are to Grau merely forms of evil, the whole human dilemma of how one handles or copes with evil. Though her characters live in and are native to the South, they remain people facing the same eternal problem of evil, a problem both literature and religion acknowledge as common to all mankind. Even though Grau is Unitarian in religious affiliation, she says that she "decided a long time ago that I was sort of fundamentalist oriented . . . maybe it's emotional rather than rational, but there's something very aesthetically satisfying in the shape of sin, redemption, and so on. The theology is just awful! But the ideas that one sometimes believes in, they've been around a long time now; they just have their names changed. Most people put Freudian names to these things, but they're the same basic ideas. I don't think you deal with what you were; Flannery O'Connor, for example, did so only after she went on a Catholic kick."[30]

Race and religion clearly form a part of the elusive category of "Southern" writer, but only a part; if any label were to be placed on Grau as an artist, it would be as one with a strong sense of "place," an emphasis in her work, as will be noted in greater detail in later chapters, on the locale in which her work is set and the identification the reader has with that locale. Hence calling Grau a "Southern" writer is appropriate, but not for the facile reason of mere geographic setting or residence; rather, her entire life has been spent with a self-conscious awareness of locale. As a child, as mentioned earlier, her family divided its time between Alabama and New Orleans; as a young writer just out of college, she divided her time between residence in New Orleans and visiting New York; as a wife and mother she and her family divide their time between New Orleans and Martha's Vineyard. "Somehow," she says, "my family has always lived in two places. I don't really know why."[31]

New Orleans especially is a paradox to Grau, a place reflecting opposite tendencies. "It's a place where nobody really bothers. They're hung up on being free and easy. Nobody in New Orleans cares. . . . And they don't know about such things as literature. In fact, I actually don't think most of my acquaintances even know I write. We don't talk about it. It isn't nice—women simply don't work in the South."[32] In her youth, New Orleans was considered the "only really civilized city in the South," even though it was a city of decay combined with charm. "Now it has lost three-fourths of its character, and there is very little left except drunken Texans in the French Quarter. And yet, I sort of like the corrupt tone of the city. There's a certain appeal. I can't explain it. . . . But for the most part, New Orleans has become a minus city" and is "actively hostile to intellectualism," while it clings to an "image that wasn't valid in the first place."[33] In 1964 she said, "we're all influenced a great deal by what we read, but—good heavens— there's little of it in New Orleans—in the South. I just looked up the publishers' sales figures and they're fantastic. Louisiana was right at the bottom. I wouldn't have believed it would edge out South Carolina. But it did."[34]

Still, it is always back to New Orleans following vacations in the North, and it remains the South that Grau deals with, especially the Gulf Coast locales that predominate in her work. As will be seen, there is little in her work to link her with other "Southern" writers except for setting, and for her repeated emphasis on the evil that lies within man as that evil struggles against good. Her simultaneous liking and disliking the South seems analogous to this ethical tension between good and evil—not as a mere facile object lesson about the indominatability of good, but much more as profound examination of the appeal of evil in man's life.

A regional writer such as Grau must also be distinguished from a purely "local color" writer.[35] Grau's Gulf-Coast South is an integral part of her life and of the lives of her characters, not mere "window-dressing" for a quaint, picturesque landscape. That is, most of Grau's characters sense the importance of the place in which they live, as well as the importance of family traditions and relationships, patterns of behavior and thinking and speaking, and their very perception of their world. More than any other part of the country, the South—if one can speak of it monolithically for a moment—seems to have resisted change the most doggedly and persistently, handing down, generation to generation, the truths of the past that ostensibly remain immutable and sacred. Hence the regional writer does not create nostalgic settings for their own sake so much as to create authentic backgrounds against which his characters are seen in perspective; in such a case the setting is less important than the genuineness of the people portrayed as existing within that setting—and this is a far cry from the clichéd antebellum South that inevitably becomes the trite expression of everything that is "Southern" in the local-colorist's mind. Grau's authentic regionalism, then, is not only valid in its own terms, it also does not overwhelm her characters and the deeper issues that govern their behavior. As will be noted in more detail further in this study, Grau reflects the qualities of a regional novelist at their best.

III   *Grau's Ideas About Writing*

Unlike some novelists who prefer not to offer comments about their craft—possibly clinging to the idea that to discuss their creativity would in some way diminish it—Grau has offered numerous comments about her intentions and techniques, even though these could by no means be considered a sustained theory of the craft of writing. Rather, she has attempted to suggest some of the thinking that led to her writing her various novels and stories. Out of this have come not only the novels and stories themselves, which after all are her chief concern, but also a few more general remarks about the process of writing itself; comments regarding the writing of specific novels are included in the respective chapters of this book.

In an essay entitled "The Essence of Writing," Grau begins by saying, "Me give advice about writing? Good heavens, no." Disarming though this might be, she goes on to qualify her statement by in fact offering just such advice. A writer, she says, is one who has developed a "certain facility with words," a facility shared by such others as con men, real estate agents, and teachers. This common quality obviously transcends esoteric working habits, and in her own case, with a house and family to take care of, she simply cannot afford "fixed habits" of composition, so much of her writing has been done under less-than-ideal circumstances, with children and dogs competing for attention. Hence she says that writing classes, for example, are useful because they force a person to discipline himself: "To put something down on paper, good or bad—that is the beginner's most difficult problem. If a writing class compels him to produce, if it makes him feel guilty about not writing—well, that's a good class."

For herself, Grau likes the "isolation, the mental freedom to explore the bewildering behavior of Homo sapiens." And she likes to wonder at "the unanswered puzzle of all successful works of fiction: *Why is success not really a matter of skill?*" (Grau's emphasis). Hence she spends half her time, she says, simply trying to learn the secrets of other writers and then to apply them to her own writing. This, then, is the "essence of writing": she feels that she must comment on man and his world; she wants to systematize the way a philosopher does; she wants, in brief, to make the "muddle of human life" more understandable and bearable than it would otherwise be. Preachy though this is, Grau does believe that a writer is a sort of evangelist "whose preaching is extremely subtle and utterly disguised—quite possibly even from himself." His view of the world around him is therefore constantly shifting, because "fiction at its best is a mirror of that constantly changing reality."

On a more down-to-earth level, she adds, the day-to-day life of a writer is a series of "problem-solving experiments in words," with these problems including his thinking of himself as "a storyteller, a mood-evoker, a delineator of character." And as a storyteller, which Grau primarily thinks she is, she utilizes places and events she has known in her own life without this ever becoming autobiographical, or a combination of things she has experienced and read about, or simple incidents she has observed that become the essence of a story. And all of this results in "an endless unraveling of ideas, and endless exploration of the possibilities of life."[36]

And then, on an even more practical level, Grau revises everything she writes at least three times before it is published. Despite what may appear merely unnecessary rewriting, Grau continues to believe that writing is "lots of fun."[37] She normally takes a year and a half or so mulling over an idea for a novel before she writes any of it, and then, seeing as she does that writing is "a series of problems to be solved not by flashes of insight but by steady, rational application," she tells a story. She has "never researched anything" in her life, she claims, but she does put together the "repository of odd bits of tales accumulated over the years from all kinds of places: newspapers, family stories, gossip. I remember and call on the information when I need it." This necessarily rules out, as already suggested, set work hours (which to her seems a kind of "foolish, arbitrary organization"); she simply works as much as she needs to, seldom more than three or four hours a day, either when her children are at school or late at night. "It's better to write every day once a book is started. It's easier then . . . you don't lose the thread."[38] And as she approaches her self-imposed deadline, she picks up speed and simply completes the work.

The academic year 1969–1970, during which Grau taught creative writing at the University of New Orleans, enabled her to try to put some of these thoughts in the concrete form required for the classroom situation. She says that she does not know what value such classes have except for the fact that they force people to write, a form of discipline that makes the student put something on paper. One thing she hopes her students learned from her is that "writing isn't just a matter of expressing" oneself. Rejecting the narcissistic tendency of our day in which people think that merely because something interests them it will therefore interest others as well, Grau says that "aspiring writers must learn that writing is making a structure, and it is putting thoughts into that structure for the total effect."[39]

Creativity, she believes, is an "abstract thing" foreign to her nature: "We invariably fall so short of what we're trying to achieve, because the language just doesn't carry with a subject like that [i.e., the creative process]."[40] The reason, she says, is that "we don't have the vaguest idea about creativity. . . . Either you have the desire to create or you don't. We walk or we fall."[41] Regarding writing as a craft as she does, as "something to be worked at very hard,"[42] she believes that such creative writing courses, while they will not automatically make a person into a writer, can "bring out latent talent and prod one into writing." Indeed, her systematic, intelligent manner of doing the required writing for John Husband's class at Tulane University is what he attributes as the reason for her success: "She told me then she had made up her mind to be a writer and wanted to do all the work that was necessary and learn all that was necessary to achieve this goal."[43] Needless to say, she is her own best testimonial to the validity of her statements regarding the craft of writing.

CHAPTER 2

The Hard Blue Sky

G RAU'S first novel, *The Hard Blue Sky*, was published in 1958 to
a generally enthusiastic critical reception. Those readers and
reviewers who had seen in *The Black Prince and Other Stories* the
signs of a promising literary career were not disappointed, and the
book went into several cloth-bound printings and repeated paperback
editions. Portions of the book, in somewhat different form, had
appeared previously in the *New Yorker* (September 24, 1955), *New
World Writing* (Tenth Mentor Selection, 1956), and *Mademoiselle*
(September, 1957); but isolated portions of the novel could not prepare
readers for the impact of the entire work.

I *Setting*

Set among the islands south of New Orleans, between Barataria Bay
and the Gulf of Mexico, *The Hard Blue Sky* primarily concerns some
thirty-odd fishermen and their families, all of Cajun lineage, who
occupy Isle aux Chiens; to a lesser extent, an indeterminate number of
oyster men, primarily of Yugoslav ancestry, who occupy the island of
Terre Haute; and a few townsfolk on the mainland and in New Orleans. Grau has stated that she did not have any specific islands in mind
when she wrote the novel:

The names are fictitious; . . . it's sort of a composite island, Grand Isle, where
we went summers when we were children, directly across the Mississippi
river and straight down; it's officially part of Jefferson Parish [county], this
parish we're in. The Isle of Dogs, the name it had in the book, is more or less
Grand Isle when I was little. In those days it was a fisherman's island, whereas
now it's all oil rigs; in those days there were no oil rigs, just fishermen. This
island in the book is the Grand Isle I remember, plus a few other
islands. . . . [1]

Grau's explicitness about the setting is significant because the novel, above all, is integrally intertwined with setting. Indeed, setting can be singled out as the work's primary focus, even more than the lives and actions of the many characters in the work. And as if to emphasize this for the reader's benefit, Grau includes a four-page introductory essay about the locale, almost as if the details provided, in lieu of a map, were taken from a notebook used for the writing of the novel. Emphasized in this brief opening statement are such facts as the gradually diminishing land area as a result of the gulf's constant erosion, the fauna of the islands, details about each of the several islands, and comments about the inhabitants' ancestry and insular existence on Isle aux Chiens, going back even to stories of pirates such as Jean Lafitte: "But that was back before anyone's memory. Even prohibition was a long time past. And the money from it was gone years ago" (7)[2]. The people of Isle aux Chiens, then, reflect a highly isolated social grouping, one that is suspicious of strangers, prone to feuding with the shrimp and oyster men of Terre Haute, inclined to avoid the mainland, and, depending upon the vagaries of the fishing season, barely above the poverty level. Their lives are their boats, and in time of storm the boats come before family or home. Indeed, so imbued are Grau's characters with a sense of honor developed over many generations that it seems likely old affronts and offenses would never be forgotten—or forgiven.

II   Regional Values and Atmosphere

As already suggested, it is easy to label Grau, as a result of *The Hard Blue Sky* and some of her later books, as a "local color" writer of the sort who uses geographic setting as window-dressing for a tale that could be set anywhere with only a slight change in clothing or accent. Such touristic writing is not, however, the kind that Grau provides in *The Hard Blue Sky*; it is regional writing, to be sure, but this does not imply a pejorative diminishing of the talent necessary to render the locale so vividly that it becomes a universal experience. The values identified with the "primitive" inhabitants of her coastal islands are not lessened but rather enhanced through her narration—values such as family loyalty, vengeance, social conduct, the natural passage from birth to death, and, above all, a stoical acceptance of the inevitable. In both life and in nature, this stoicism becomes an overwhelming determinant of character interaction and survival; Grau's people survive catastrophic storms and family tragedies just as they do the uncertain, whimsical fishing season. One is tempted to compare this with Faulkner's statement about his characters' ability to "endure," but there is a difference in that Grau's people do not seem to overcome their difficulties, even if this results from patience and a sense of moral rightness, as with Faulkner's Dilsey; Grau's characters simply continue, more or less passively accepting whatever happens, but seeming to gain no moral victory over their environment or antagonists. Hence the kind of regionalism utilized by Grau differs significantly from that loosely identified with other "Southern" writers such as Faulkner.

Furthermore, Grau does not depend on some of the types of picturesque details some regional writers use, such as quaintness of setting in time or emphasis on certain traditions. Her characters in *The Hard Blue Sky*, while possibly not memorable as individuals, do not reflect the lives of their forebears and the similar struggles they have previously experienced; these characters, again, simply *accept* what they are given, and as a consequence rarely look at their world and their lives in critical perspective. Some of the flora on Isle aux Chiens, for example, could well be considered picturesque—wisteria, hibiscus, bougainvillea, oleanders, all the rest. But the necessity of struggling to stay alive, and the total indifference to much more than talking and drinking beer and dancing and occasionally making love when not working, suggests that these people are tuned in to the high-and-low rhythms of daily existence and the natural sequence of the seasons, not to anything more analytical or inquiring. The routine is unvarying and from a more sophisticated perspective rather monotonous; for the men, the routine usually consists of listening to ballgames on the radio and getting drunk on Saturday nights, and for the women and children it is the once-a-month visit from an indifferent priest. Life merely goes on; and the older inhabitants, such as Mamere Terrebonne (itself a suggestive name meaning literally "Mother Good-Earth"), have seen so many repetitions of the patterns of birth, growing up, mating, and dying that little surprises them. Aside from various recent introductions such as electricity and the telephone, little seems to have changed in generations, and thus a stoical acceptance of *what is* becomes the way of life for most of the residents.

And paramount among the numerous details of setting, of the island's heritage and present degree of diminished glory, is the atmosphere itself. The novel's title suggests a unique kind of sky that is as difficult to capture in words as, say, is that of El Greco's Toledo. Grau, however, emphasizes the atmosphere (and, correspondingly, the weather) throughout the entire novel, making this the single most important element in the lives of the characters and in the reader's consideration. The first words of Grau's introductory essay about the islands mention the times when "the sun is very clear and the sky a hard blue" (3), and toward the novel's close, when Mamere Terrebonne studies the sky, looking for a sign that will tell her what lies ahead, she sees a "winter-colored sky," a portent of death, a sky that is "very high and very blue and very hard" (438). Grau is certainly not original in using the pervasive, blistering sun as symbolically suggestive of an enervating existence. One can think offhand of such other examples as Camus's *The Stranger* and Gide's *The Immoralist,* in both of which a comparable use of the burning sun leads to an indifference, both physical and moral, to normal human values. This does not, however, diminish Grau's skillful integration of sky and clouds and storm into the lives of her characters.

When asked about the preponderance of atmospheric details such as these, Grau replied: "On the gulf you're darned exposed, a little old sand speck, so you're terribly aware of the sound of the waves and the way the wind is blowing. Any sea coastal resident is aware immediately of a change in the wind."[3] And most exposed of all, in a sense, is a woman like Mamere Terrebonne, who knows her end is coming. She significantly has the shutters on her house attached tightly after observing the hard, blue sky, for she knows that both the winter of the year and the winter of her life are approaching, and that such preparations are necessary. Grau commented that what strikes her about the people on the Gulf Coast is their ability "to go back to the same spot and start life over again, almost like ants building," and that such actions on the part of Mamere Terrebonne are typical among peasants in other places in the world as well: "It's a normal occurrence that old people die. They have a certain belief in the inevitability of life and death. . . . We're pretty well pressured in cities to decorate everything over, so anything foreign to our experience is covered, everything neatly covered up. I seem to favor old people, don't I? . . . The whole point of their lives is that it *didn't* matter what happened."[4]

III   *The Characters and Their Stories*

The foregoing may suggest that an old one such as Mamere Terrebonne is a central figure in the novel instead of the symbolic oracle that she is. In fact, *The Hard Blue Sky* primarily consists of two distinct, interrelated stories (as are almost all the people on the Isle aux

Chiens), both about young people in their teens and twenties and their parents' generation as well. The focal character in the novel is surely young Annie Landry, and the events that occur in her life during the hot, humid summer that comprises the time period covered by the novel are the central ones in the book. Annie, just turned sixteen, is a restless, rootless adolescent, bored but not sure what she is bored with. In the course of the novel, her father, Al, a widower, meets and marries Adele, from the mainland, further alienating Annie from any sense of community with him. Annie, like the other idle young people on the island, is drawn to a new and sleek sloop that ties up at the island while the rich owner and his toothache-prone wife return to New Orleans; left to care for the *Pixie* is Inky D'Alfonso, the one-man crew. Inky, relatively sophisticated by island standards, is only reluctantly accepted by the island's inhabitants since he is an outsider; but Annie finds him appealing. Annie has had one sexual encounter before Inky, with Perique Lombas, an older teenager who took her in his rough, drunken manner and who does not even recall the incident.

With Inky, however, Annie gradually finds a more appealing romantic and sexual relationship, and at the novel's conclusion they go off together to New Orleans. As a younger adolescent, Annie had spent ten unhappy months at a convent in that city, and therefore finds the appeal of leaving the island ultimately irresistible. Inky has as his avocation drawing pencil drawings of nudes, to sell to tourists in New Orleans for five dollars each, and Annie becomes not only his lover (a fact the islanders accept like any other event in life—passively and stoically) but also his model and eventually his wife. Since Annie is ready for whatever occurs in life, she is never surprised at changes of circumstance or fate, nor does she get deeply involved in the decision-making process. Hence leaving with Inky is neither better nor worse than staying on the island she has always known, just different. And she is ready for the new life with Inky. As it turns out, based on how one reads the conclusion to the novel, she may well have chosen the only means of staying alive.

The other central story in the novel concerns the Livaudais family, especially the teenage boys Henry and Pete. Henry leaves for a hunting trip into the marshes, but fails to return. His family, more disturbed over his not being found than the fact that he may be dead, searches fruitlessly for several days. Then one of the residents from the island of Terre Haute, an old Yugoslav shrimpman, comes to talk to the elder Livaudais to inform him that Henry has run away with a girl from his own family. Since the couple has chosen a dangerous route to escape the two communities, the old man merely wants to be able to claim whatever is left of the girl if the two young people turn up dead.

Pete Livaudais, more hot-headed than careful, sneaks over to Terre Haute with cans of gasoline, and sets fire to buildings on that island. He and his family know that retribution is likely, and so they guard their boats night and day. But the Terre Haute residents come to Isle aux Chiens by a different route, and set fire to several unguarded homes, including Annie's. Only another family's home is destroyed, however, but the implication is clear that the feud will have many more manifestations of violence before tempers are cooled. The fact that the reprisals and violence occur toward the novel's end is not surprising, for the atmospheric details that twine through the novel tell increasingly that a hurricane is imminent; the violence of nature thus has its counterpart in the violence of mankind. And as the storm strikes the island, the men take their boats out of its path to safety, while the women and children prepare to wait out the storm.

But Grau is ambiguous at the novel's end: is the reader to assume that after the storm life will continue as it has for so long, or is this storm the one that will wipe out the island permanently? After all, we are told, early in the novel, when Inky first appears, that the storms continually take more than their toll. Annie mentions that the Rendezvous, a tavern, was not always on the beach, as it is now, but that there were formerly a number of oaks between the building and the beach; the water constantly encroaches and takes away pieces of land. As Annie says: " 'Pieces of the beach goes all the time, with the water sucking away at it. And when it comes to a hurricane, big chunks of it goes. All the trees that used to be out here went with one of them, my papa says. And it wasn't no time till the sand moved up, right up to the porch' " (24). When asked about the ambiguous ending, about whether the island is destroyed totally and entirely, or that the people return and life goes on as before, Grau replied: "I think . . . that it probably didn't matter."[5] Again, as with the sense of inevitability mentioned earlier, Grau seems to say that to the people on the island there is little difference—life or death, island or no islands, homes or no homes, all existence is on a continuum of indifference. Artistically, too, an ambiguous ending is most effective; Grau comments that she did not see beyond the ending of the book, and one might deduce from this that the same ambiguity exists regarding the other questions one raises as the book is read: Do Annie and Inky, for instance, survive happily as a married couple? Is further feuding between the two inhabited islands likely after the hurricane sweeps through both communities with presumably awesome damage? And so on. The ending is as stark and as bare as the receding shoreline following each new onslaught from nature.

IV *Narrative Techniques*

Grau's narrative technique in *The Hard Blue Sky* is consistently straightforward and relatively free of stylistic or structural experimentation. Aside from a self-conscious use of flashback to provide expository details about various characters as they are introduced or emphasized in the novel, she maintains a consistently sequential series of incidents. For example, when Mamere Terrebonne is first introduced wandering near the island's sole store, we are given a digressive account of an illness she had had two years previously, followed by a contrived reference to Mamere not being related to the Livaudais clan as a means of shifting the narrative to them. And when Annie first enters the narrative as a significant figure, we are given a lengthy flashback to her ten months' stay at the Ursuline convent in New Orleans, the same one Grau herself attended. Such an account could be given as well in purely expository background sections of the novel prior to Annie's active role in the life of the island. But Grau's technique, though not at all subtle, prepares us for the conflicts in Annie's life, just as the several pages devoted to Mamere Terrebonne help the reader to sense the place she will play in the ultimate activities on Isle aux Chiens.

In Annie's case, her stay in the convent clearly shows her sexual frustration and clinical curiosity: she has as roommate a private, reclusive South American girl named Beatriz. In time Annie discovers that Beatriz sneaks out at night for a liaison with an unnamed young man. Annie's curiosity and perhaps morbid interest in discovering their activities leads her to climb around the entire building on the window sill, high above the ground, and then to edge her way around to where Beatriz and her lover are. Unable to see the couple, Annie climbs to the building's roof and jubilantly, headily senses her status high above all others in her world. She painfully and methodically returns to her room, with but one regret: she did not get to see Beatriz and her lover after all. In time she leaves the convent, realizing that she has learned but three things while there: to chant, to embroider, and to crochet.

One might add as well: to cry, for she thereafter, for reasons not clear to her, begins weeping.

A reason does exist, however, and upon her return to the island we see that it is her father's new interest in Adele—and again there is a flashback to the life Adele, a widow, with a small son, has had in the town of Port Ronquille. Combined with Annie's sexual longings is her incipient jealousy caused by her father's new bride. Earlier that summer Perique had forced his sexual attentions on Annie, in what could only be described as a drunken rape, leaving Annie more afraid, confused, and surprised than hurt—or satisfied.

An incident in which Annie's suppressed feelings are especially made vivid relates to her longings in her dreams for escape from the mundane life on the island. Grau is not a writer who uses overt symbolism with frequency or, for that matter, with deliberate attention to repetition of patterns of imagery. But Annie has one especially clear dream that causes her to whimper and toss in her sleep, with the recurring symbol of "three balls, yellow, bright yellow each one; she could see them rolling across the ground" (121). Only later, in the flashback providing the reader with information about Annie's stay in the convent, do we realize what she has been dreaming of. Once, when she was ten, she had accompanied her mother and great-aunt to Holy Week services at the cathedral in New Orleans: "She hadn't been more than ten then, so small that she had to stand on the pew to get one glimpse of the altar: three gold domes sparkling under dozens of candles" (126). We can conclude, without stretching this interpretation too far, that Annie's childish fascination with the elegant trappings of the cathedral service becomes submerged in the most vivid of the sights during the service, the three golden domes, and that as she grows older this one dimly remembered experience takes on the aura of a form of escape from the extremely mundane, poverty-level existence that life on the island offers. Annie's rebelling against the conventional mores of the island comes to a head when she whimperingly dreams of the same golden domes she had seen on an earlier "escape." Ironically, she is the slowest to mature of the adolescent girls on the island; at the time she is having the nightmare, her aunt is complaining about her not wearing a bra, and her frustrated incipient sexual longings combine with these other impulses in her life to lead to a state of discontent. Throughout most of the balance of the novel, Annie is either secluded in her own private worlds (in the midst of a thicket of bushes, for example, or merely daydreaming or reading), or involved with Inky, who represents for her the glorious world "out there." Even though the *Pixie* is his own by virtue of his having to stay with it while the owner languishes in New Orleans, it does represent a means of escape—and this need to escape is heightened all the more by her father's new family, Adele and her son.

Grau, though, does not allow the reader to make such symbolic and thematic connections often in this novel. For the most part the book is concerned with the climatic effects mentioned earlier. Related to such effects, however, is her excellent use of sensory details, notably the synesthetic use of overlapping sensory details. For example, Grau tells of Inky's initial arrival in the wharf area of Isle aux Chiens by noting that the assembled children smelled to him like peanuts, followed by his sense that the water around the boat had a "faint sweet-sour smell," accompanied by the appearance of being "dark with an almost oily surface," and with a dryness in his throat that implies sunstroke. In this entire passage Grau repeatedly emphasizes such sensory details, especially those identified with the sense of smell: varnished wood, perfume, sweat, paint, tar, the stuffiness of an enclosed room on the boat in the hot midday sun (38–39). When Annie offers Inky a room at her house, she emphasizes the smell of the turtles and rabbits her cousin, who had once had the room, had kept there (43).

Similarly, later in the novel, we are told the background of Julius Arceneux, who runs the island's only store: years earlier, when he had gone to town to propose marriage to the young woman he had seen at mass, he barely dares to breathe in the priest's house because he is so "upset" by the smells of town houses: kerosene, greens, fish, and the "sweet-like odor of mice in the walls" (67). Julius, if we are to believe the narrative, is a paragon of auditory sensitivity; as a child, he is said to be able to hear not only the "squack of birds, the bumble of insects . . . , and the slither of snakes," but also the very movement of ants and even the sound of roots growing (55)!

In all these cases—and they could be multiplied endlessly in the novel—Grau demonstrates a sharp, sensitive handling of sensory detail, with such detail often contributing integrally to the impact of a character's evaluation of a setting or situation in which he finds himself. True, Grau uses all the senses in such description, but it seems clear that the sense of smell is the most keenly depended upon in the novel. When asked about this use of smell, Grau claimed that it was not deliberate,[6] but clearly such a proliferation of olfactory images suggests a studied—and successful—kind of artistry.

V *Evaluation*

As a novel, *The Hard Blue Sky* is less successful as an intricately counterpointed plot than it is as a series of episodic tableaux, individual set pieces tied in with one or the other of the two central stories; some of these individual episodes could easily have been developed as short stories or even as novels in their own right instead of serving as variations on the theme of the book, i.e., that the people in the islands face both good and bad in life with a stoical acceptance of the inevitable. The overall effect is rich and synesthetic, but the concluding events in the book are both predictable and inevitable, given the premise of all that has occurred previously in the novel. That is, the reader is not surprised at Annie's going off with Inky any more than he is at the climatic events likely to cause imminent destruction; there is no necessary causal relationship among the events in the book, because, like the unpredictable weather always affecting whatever the characters might do, things merely happen.

While the book may not be so episodic as to appear a mere collage of incidents or even a quasi-picaresque work (with no single person but rather all those on the island merely wandering and waiting), it is, as has been claimed, rather "aimless" in that Grau "seems less concerned about what her characters do than the background against which they do it."[7] The emphasis on atmosphere, one of the book's admittedly strong points, serves both to illustrate the characters' great dependence on and relationship to the natural order, and to lead the reader to feel that these characters are primitives, people indifferently and uniformly accepting all that life offers, from death to sex to hurricane to drinking beer to observing the changing of the seasons. That is, little if anything causes any heightening of awareness or greater-than-normal sensitivity to the dramatic events that distinguish one day from the next, or their own lives from the more sedate lives of those on the mainland.

True, Grau does not patronize her characters, primitives though they may be;[8] but she similarly does not enter fully into their consciousnesses in such a way as to allow the reader to know how they *feel* about the spectrum of human experience, or whether their true responses are different from their somewhat stoical indifference to guilt or responsibility. As Annie Landry reflects as she leaves the island to marry Inky, "Things happened . . . and you did whatever it was you had to do to meet them. And they went on past you. . . . She was waiting, waiting for things to happen to her. Things that could be handled and changed" (427).

But such change is neither desired by these islanders, nor welcomed when it is forcibly intruded upon their complacent existences, and even Annie, although leaving the island, presumably forever, seems unmoved by the dramatic change in her own circumstances. Perhaps she will indeed escape the fate of her fellow islanders, though one doubts this, given all that we have already seen and heard of Annie. It may well be that another of the young women on the island, Cecile Arcenaux, could conceivably have made such a break, but she too is trapped, with a child to care for and a family for which she has a sense of responsibility. On one occasion, Cecile sits with her child, staring at the "hard blue sky" cited so often in the novel, and as she sits and thinks, she realizes that "It don't even matter that we been alive" (287). She throws a brick futilely at the sky as she leaves, but, turning to go home, she does not even wait to see it fall. Even Cecile, though for a brief moment she has seen the unending, meaningless routine of her folk, can do nothing to fight it, not even to watch her symbolically brave but ineffectual gesture of defiance conclude with the brick falling to the ground. For even this small gesture of determination, though resulting in no substantive change in her life, is still more than Annie, who does in fact escape the island, cares to make.

Grau's strength in this novel, then, is in the cumulative effect of the sequence of incidents and the rich sense of characterization she demonstrates through relatively minor details of speech or behavior. It is a rich book, yet it "never coalesces into a unified novel,"[9] that is, a work with a clearly demarcated sequential plot that the reader feels actually concludes. No doubt this inconclusiveness is partly intentional, for the sense that life continues inexorably, even after the novel ends, is pervasive throughout the book. The novel's impact is nonetheless great, and the promise it demonstrated was fully fulfilled in the works to follow.

CHAPTER 3

The House on Coliseum Street

G RAU'S second novel, *The House on Coliseum Street,* was published to mixed reviews in June, 1961, and aside from the same
general emphasis on locale found in *The Hard Blue Sky,* little similarity exists between the two books. For one thing, *The House on Coliseum Street,* running only some 60,000 words, is a quite short novel,
and since Grau's strengths as a writer are generally more satisfactorily
realized in her short fiction than in her novels, this, the shortest by far
of her five novels, has a compactness and directness quite unlike the
others. Then, too, this work develops a theme concerning a neurotic
young woman considerably more difficult to realize than the expansive,
open confrontation of man and nature found in the earlier work.

I *The Characters and Their Story*

Joan Mitchell is the oldest of five daughters born to Aurelie Caillet,
in five successive marriages; Joan, age twenty, is two years older than
Doris, six more than Celine, eight more than Phyllis, and eleven more
than Ann. Only Joan and Doris are emphasized in the book, however,
for the younger girls spend the summer in camp and the rest of the
year in convent school and are only glimpsed once briefly in the novel.
At the time the book takes place—evidently, judging from internal references to dates, in 1959—the mother is married to Herbert Norton,
Ann's father, who has retreated to seclusion on the third floor of the
house, apart from Aurelie and the rest except for deliveries of liquor
and occasional "drying-out" spells at the Veterans Administration hospital. Joan's own father, a blond Italian from Lombardy, had died following his divorce from Aurelie, leaving Joan well fixed financially;
indeed, to some extent the entire family is supported by his estate. The
house itself is in a shabby-genteel area of New Orleans, about two miles
southeast of the French Quarter, near Audubon Park and not far from
the Tulane University–Loyola University complex on St. Charles St.;

judging from internal references, the house is evidently near Henry Clay Avenue.

Joan, who has been indifferently attending the university (which one is never specified) for two years, has equally indifferently been almost engaged to Fred Aleman, a businessman who makes love, we are told, efficiently and indifferently. Little, therefore, moves Joan, for she evinces a malaise that soon becomes considerably more clinical in intensity as a result of an impromptu liaison with Michael Kern, a young college professor. (Interestingly, Grau's husband, James Feibleman, has "Kern" as his middle name.) Kern has previously dated Doris, but the frenetic Doris, completely cynical about relationships, prefers to play games with men just as she continually plays tennis; indeed, every time she is seen in the book she is dressed for tennis. For no particular reason Joan accepts a date with Kern, spontaneously has sexual intercourse with him, and eventually finds herself pregnant by him; not surprisingly, she and Fred had always been "careful." After telling her mother of her pregnancy, Joan is sent some miles away from New Orleans for a "rest" with her aunt, who arranges an abortion; some weeks later, when Joan returns home, her depression is so great that she virtually becomes a recluse herself, in the top floors of the university library, where she works till late every night. Fred is almost forgotten, but her obsession with Kern is so great that she begins trailing him, eventually finds that he is dating a freshman (evidently against school rules), and, at the book's climax, "ruins" him by telling his dean the story not only of his current liaison but also of her own relationship with him. The novel ends with Joan, sitting in a fetus position on her doorstep (she has forgotten the key), waiting for the new day.

II *Joan's Neuroticism*

Joan's neurotic condition is the heart of the book, for Aurelie goes on from man to man as from day to day, concerned only with appearances and propriety at the moment, while Doris feverishly attempts to escape the realities of home and heritage by sports; obvious affinities exist between Aurelie and Amanda Wingfield in Tennessee Williams' *The Glass Menagerie*, just as Doris to some extent reminds the reader of Jordan Baker in Fitzgerald's *The Great Gatsby:* each is a type, and each avoids confrontation with the harshness of insecure life through conventional routine of one sort or another. Only Joan finds that routine does not work as a way to expiate her sense of guilt—not only the guilt of her aborted pregnancy (profound as this is), but perhaps even more the aborted relationships she and her sisters have had in a home lacking a secure father figure on whom they could depend when necessary. It is not surprising that Doris on more than one occasion in the book refers to the house as a "house full of bitches" (e.g., p. 171).[1] Joan, we are told, had always "wanted to get away" from the reality of the house, and when as a child she had attended camp she had not missed the house at all; it is not until she has reconciled herself to the destruction of Kern that she finds herself able to like the house—and even this implies the presence of the comfortable, safe Fred as much as her mother and sister.

Joan's guilt, as I have mentioned, is specifically tied in with her pregnancy and subsequent abortion. When she first discovered that she was pregnant, she reacted with a "Don't be silly" and attempted to evade the reality of her condition for some weeks thereafter. Sex for her had been a passive act, one lacking fervent involvement, and although we are told on several occasions that she could "smell" sex in the air, she is basically afraid of, yet curiously drawn toward, sexual activities. For example, when she is working in the library stacks, she hears a couple making love in an isolated study carrel far away from others in the library; her reaction is acute embarrassment, and she for the first time goes to chat with other library employees elsewhere on a lower stack level. Her sexual involvement with Fred, too, is evidently far from a passionate relationship:

> He talked, joked even, from the time he switched off the car engine until the instant of his shuddering climax. Then after a brief interval, he began again.
> She rather liked it. It was like having the radio on. (83)

When Kern takes her far out in the country, near where she had lived as a child, she reminisces about the clumsy lovemaking efforts of adolescence—"more pain and uncertainty than anything else, but desperately longed for and pursued" (108). Her lovemaking with Michael is considerably more spontaneous than with Fred, with an almost idyllic initial encounter under dense pine trees leading to Joan's strong sense of arousal at the very sight of Michael in the days to come:

> I wonder if he knew I wanted him as much as I did. I wouldn't like him to know.
> And it's so silly. Body running away with you like this. Running you so fast

you can't sleep. And all you can think of is the mark of a man. The stupid silly mark of a man. (164)

But when Michael begins his affair with the freshman girl, Joan radically undergoes a change, almost a change in which she wishes to hurt both herself and Michael. She believes that her own "hurt" will end when she is again pregnant and she regrets that it is necessary to have a man involved at all in insemination; then she eagerly takes the initiative in her relationship with Fred, no longer ashamed of going to his apartment, no longer caring, not even bothering to use her contraceptive.

But all this time Joan has been aware of her guilt from the abortion—not the moral aspects as such so much as the self-induced guilt arising from the thought that the tissue removed from her in the operation was little more than a minute piece of red seaweed. For the first time we are told of her nightmarish dreams, dreams in which she envisions herself filling the world with children, "like meteors flying off a sun" (217), all following in the steps of that first aborted one, the child she several times calls her "ghost child": "I could stand anything . . . if it wasn't so lonely. If I could get pregnant again, I wouldn't be so lonely. At least not for that time. There'd be two everywhere I went then, for a while" (241). All the while, Joan tries to avoid facing the future, and even goes to the extent of deliberately hurting herself emotionally by telling Fred, a little earlier in the novel, that she would not miss spending her future with him.

Since the novel is basically Joan's story, all these circumstances blend to suggest certain valid conclusions about her mental makeup. She is fond of her safe, respectable Fred, but is clearly not aroused by him either as a lover or as a person. Michael is more dangerous (since his career could be ruined, presumably, by his dating a student) and therefore more enticing and appealing. She rids herself of the child she and Michael accidentally conceive, and in time rids herself as well of him, first by destroying his later relationship with the freshman girl, then by going to the dean's house in the middle of the night to tell a fabricated tale of Michael's "immoral" involvements, even putting the blame on him for arranging her abortion. Her paranoid obsession with punishing Michael takes such forms as following him and the freshman girl throughout the city, watching his apartment, writing an anonymous letter to the girl, as well as telling all to the dean.

She is trying in her obsessed manner, therefore, to have Michael, yet not to have him; she is aroused by the very thought of him, yet she knows that he is far less "safe" for her than is Fred. This is why she tries deliberately to figure out why she is waiting so eagerly for something, without knowing what it is, at least not acknowledging to herself what it is (173). In such cases, she finds a "way out":

Whenever she felt the quivering shaking uncertainty coming near her, she would go off by herself, where there was no one to hear. And she would say her little story out loud, using the crudest words she could think of. Sometimes she made up the images, graphic ones that struck her imagination. She told the whole thing aloud to herself. The quivering would stop and she would feel better. She would feel fine. (191)

All of this, not surprisingly, is self-delusion, because it is not until she has done all the damage to Michael she can that she returns home, relatively content to be there again—but, interestingly, locked out because she had forgotten her key. She knows that she will have to leave home because of the lies she has told regarding Michael, and this is a kind of parallel lockout. But what is most intriguing in her being locked out of her house on Coliseum Street—described on the last page of the novel—is the fetal position which she assumes in the porch chair.

III   The Theme of Redemption and Rebirth

Grau has stated that her intent in the novel was to deal with sin and redemption and "everything else one identifies with fundamentalism."[2] Even though neither Joan nor anyone else in the book is described as being a member of a fundamentalist church, Grau believes that the sense of sin pervades her South. Even though Joan's actions "deliberately cut herself off" from her mother and the others, her behavior is "induced by her background; this is something she has to work her way through." Grau says that she "intended to emphasize the redemption theme; perhaps I didn't make this point strongly enough, in the last chapter. Then she's faded out, and then, in her borrowed sweater, sitting there, she has worked herself out of it in that she's made it impossible for herself to stay. She'll be hounded out, by the law, basically. People back themselves into things, and their actions are determined, perhaps not by other people, but by themselves."[3] It is almost too easy to say that Joan has been "given no models for love" and that she therefore reacts neurotically because she cannot "cope with the truth that she has fallen futilely in love."[4] It is true enough that her home has been one totally lacking in roots and family security, and that she similarly finds the world of education one of sham and pretense, as when Michael says discovery of their affair would result in his being fired. His motive in offering marriage when he is told of her pregnancy may seem mere expedient gallantry, but it does suggest a commitment between Joan and Michael qualitatively different from and better than the one she shares with Fred.

In a sense, of course, each of these lovers—and the dean as well, no doubt—becomes a kind of vicarious father figure for Joan, but her sterility springs more from a lack of concerted activity, it seems, than from cheap-shot Freudianism. Joan is considerably more introspective than either her sister (all activity) or her mother (all facade and respectability) happens to be, and pondering the alternatives in her life, none of which seems promising or appealing, leads her to perform an act of betrayal against the one person she is described as having loved. Her world may well be irresponsible and morally relativistic, but it is not lacking in potential for personal commitment.

Indeed, Joan's vicarious identification with her aborted child parallels to some extent her own father's "betrayal" (by leaving her home and then dying) of herself; her strong desire for another child—implicitly suggested by her deliberately discontinuing the use of her diaphragm when she makes love with Fred—suggests a wholeness not otherwise found in her life. Even Fred, dull, predictable Fred, becomes an appealing alternative—but only after she has exorcised all that remains of her relationship with Michael— to Michael himself. It is not deliberate revenge that she seeks regarding Michael so much as the same unconscious "disposal" of him as of his child.

And, once this has occurred, she can begin to build in a positive sense on the bodies of those she leaves behind—including her own family, whom she knows will now be so shocked at her actions in contacting Michael's dean that she will be forced to leave home. It hardly seems meaningless that the last scene in the book is one in which Joan, sitting in a fetal position, first tries futilely to open the door to the house on Coliseum Street, then notices once again the fountain built by her father in front of the house, and finally notices the sun beginning to rise. A new day has dawned for Joan, a day in which potential happiness is imminent, but surely not a day in which conventional satisfaction with anyone in her previous "world" seems likely. Grau's statement that the last couple of paragraphs deal with rebirth seems to be

exactly on target, as is her observation that the novel ends on an
upbeat, and that the ending suggests redemption.

For even though it appears superficially that Joan, as amoral as her
family and as mechanical as Fred, destroys the only imaginative alternative her life has experienced, thus suggesting that she is doomed to
perpetual neurosis and loneliness, it is really more accurate to say that
Joan's expiation for her actions takes the only form it can, one of
attempting (evidently successfully) to rid herself of all those albatross-
like persons inhibiting and frustrating her natural impulses. Each other
person in the book has tried to use Joan for his or her own purposes,
and only as she destroys Michael's career is she able as well to destroy
her dependence on the house on Coliseum Street and all identified with
it. Off by herself, still relying on her dead father's bequest, she will be
better able to fend for herself and find whatever kind of reborn fulfillment she desires. Again, this is not the promise of a certain panacea
for all that has happened so much as the *potential* for a new life; the
fact that this was not explicitly provided in the closing pages of the
novel evidently led some reviewers and critics to comment on the continued emptiness of the entire group of persons with whom Joan
relates.

IV *Sensory Details and Atmosphere*

As with her previous book, Grau is particularly concerned with the
pervasiveness of a sense of locale, although, since *The House on Coliseum Street* is set in an urban rather than rural location, this is less
integral to the protagonist's awareness of her setting as a force determining her choices of action. That is, even though the house itself is
shabbily genteel, as is the street on which it is located, Joan has far
more options in New Orleans for changing locales as her moods shift
than had the characters in *The Hard Blue Sky*. True, the house itself,
having been the home for Joan's family for five generations, is a comfortable fact of existence, a place where she can feel at home in familiar surroundings. Yet the fact remains that she is not at home there
because her father, the one to whom she was the closest, left when she
was still young. When Joan and Michael go to Carrolton (where he
hopes to buy stuffed owls' heads), she immediately knows the directions because she had come there often when her father was alive;
merely driving through the area brings back a flood of memories of
high school dates, the furtive petting following dances, and so on. To

Joan this area is more real, it seems, than is the house in which she lives with her half-sisters and mother.

Even more obvious than the reliance upon place, however, is the heavy dependence upon sensory stimuli as reflections of inner turmoil and malaise. As in *The Hard Blue Sky*, the most frequent kind of sensory imagery in *The House on Coliseum Street* seems to be olfactory (perhaps a characteristic of sultry New Orleans): Fred reminds Joan of the smell of starch and shaving lotion; Michael's car smells of sex; when registering for summer school at the university, Joan smells sex throughout the registration hall, as men and women size each other up; the smell of camphor hits Joan a number of times—in the drugstore, walking down sidewalks, elsewhere; and the house itself in particular had a "definite" smell:

It wasn't a smell of dirt. It wasn't a smell of cooking. Or of anything in particular. It was the smell of everything. Of everything that had gone on in the house for the past hundred and twenty years. It was the smell of the people and the things. Of the living that had gone on between the walls.

The smell of the generations being born. Dying. And being laid out in the front parlor with a sprig of sweet olive from the door in their clenched hand. People left their smells behind them. . . . (230)

And as she sets out for the dean's house, after she has made up her mind to purge Michael from her system, she finally knows that the smell is "the sharp, sweet odor of rats" in the house (233), the same smell she notices in the dean's house (238).

Clearly enough, these patterns of olfactory imagery suggest incidents and changes in Joan's own life even more than they reflect the actual smells of the house. Her awareness of the smells of successive living and dying in the house surely parallels her own sense of her family's orientation toward death. She once observes that her half-sister Doris had been "death-haunted" all through her childhood (97), and the series of "deaths" in her mother's marriages, including the actual death of Herbert Norton, the current husband, are also haunting in a way. She recalls her own birth (204), which coincides with her death in her disturbed thinking, a clear parallel to the abortion she has experienced.

Similarly, a frequent allusion to climatic conditions also parallels Grau's previous novel. Indeed, one of the opening pages in this novel refers to the fact that "the sun was bright and hard and the sky was a

brilliant cloudless blue" (5). Joan frequently demonstrates a knowing
interest in the changing weather, usually paralleling her own moodi-
ness, as when a sudden squall comes to the area near her aunt's house,
during her visit for the abortion, and she passively watches it ruin playing cards and run across the table. In most cases, her awareness of the
weather occurs when she is away from New Orleans proper, as in her
trip to Carrolton with Kern, because, as with Grau's earlier novel, the
terribly exposed situation in which people living on the coast find
themselves is both more immediate and more frightening than the
likely consequences of a storm in the city. September arrives with news
of hurricanes in the gulf, and Joan is reminded of the time a large beer
sign atop a building was "ripped off like a top-heavy flower," crushing
several people (165). November's rains make her feel "terribly old,"
old enough to be the mother of the campus couples walking around
the university (203). And December causes Aurelie to flutter around
covering her flowers and in general acting more domestic than usual
(213). In these and similar cases, Joan's changing sense of identity and
self-worth seems to coincide with her acute sensitivity to the changing
seasons and their corresponding weather conditions.

V   Evaluation

The House on Coliseum Street is both an improvement upon and
a decline from Grau's achievement in *The Hard Blue Sky.* For one
thing, the relatively plotless and highly episodic *The Hard Blue Sky*
has been succeeded by a tighter novel with a more carefully structured
plot sequence, fewer unresolved loose ends, and a distinct sense of its
having ended when one finishes reading it. One senses in the earlier
novel a constant feeling of being prepared for something, though one
is never sure of exactly what, so that by the time the hurricane hits the
island, one is almost beyond accepting it as the climax to the character
tensions that fill so much of the book. But *The House on Coliseum
Street* avoids creating such unfulfilled expectations to a great extent in
that the entire book seems not only focused on one character—Joan
Mitchell—but even more concerned with her development as a character. That is, even though Joan manifests neurotic traits, she is still a
strong enough figure to tie together the idiosyncratic family of which
she is a member, as well as the few male hangers-on who move in and
out of the story. And at the novel's end, it is Joan who clearly remains
the protagonist and whose future we continue to find potentially fas-

cinating. By contrast, it is doubtful whether many readers of *The Hard Blue Sky* wondered for long at the novel's end, as the hurricane is imminent, whether Annie and Inky will live happily ever after; in the midst of so many vigorous individual characters, these two simply merge into the outside world, leaving the islanders to fend for themselves during the storm.

There are, as has been noted, similarities between Annie and Joan, similarities which apply as well to a number of Grau's subsequent female protagonists:

> . . . an intermittent disposition to sever connections with immediate reality in favor of hallucination or "trance"; a rather dumb passivity; an apparent tendency to "stalk" lovers at night; a strong desire for sex which, when it comes, seems rather flat and dull. . . . Both girls, finally, come to us as *given;* they act credibly enough, on the whole, but the reportage is so external that one never feels the necessity for their actions. . . . A certain dull opacity of character seems to spill over into their characterizations. . . .[5]

There is, moreover, a considerably greater effort to probe into Joan's mind and sensitivity than there was with the earlier young woman. While literary psychoanalyzing may have its merits, there is no need to speculate wildly in Joan's case; most of Joan's malaise stems from the guilt—self-induced or socially inspired, whichever the case may be—she experiences following her abortion. It is, significantly, an act that is never discussed or mentioned by anyone in the family after it occurs, almost as if it never happened or was considered so déclassé that no one would dare allude to it without fear of having violated both social decorum and personal privacy.

The abortion itself seemed to Joan to be one of these unmentionable but necessary situations from which one had to extricate oneself as carefully as possible. She felt no particular guilt over the operation itself, but in the months following the abortion, she increasingly is obsessed with her "seaweed child," as she calls it; in particular, thoughts of the unborn child come to her when she prepares to write the letter to Michael's new love, the freshman college student:

> The rain made her feel terribly old. Old enough to be their [i.e., college-aged couples walking through the rain] mother. Old enough to be through with the hot drive of mating. . . .
> Her mood changed. She was no longer impenetrable; she was light. Easy and drifting.

I can remember, she thought, when I was born. A lot of swirling waters
and a beat like surf pounding.

And do you remember dying afterwards? Like that. Slipping in and out of
life. And did an embryo remember dying? Did my seaweed child remember?
Drifting and surf pounding.

Empty inside and lonesome. Caverns and caves, echoing. The Holy Ghost
now. Or the Shower of Gold. . . .

Being one is so lonesome. With another heart ticking away inside. A different beat. A ragged pattern. The little ticking heart. The soft floating seaweed bones. . . . (203–204)

Though one might speculate about why Joan acts as she does, especially regarding writing to the dean to "ruin" Michael, she seems, as
this lengthy quotation and other illustrations of the same recurring
motif indicate, clearly to be acting both out of guilt for what she has
done and out of frustration at the total emotional emptiness of her life.
No doubt the warped sense of "love" leading to her mother's five marriages and her sister's repeated liaisons apply to some extent, for Joan
seems simply incapable of total commitment to either Fred or to
Michael—and, presumably, to anyone else happening upon the scene
as well. She stands to gain nothing as a result of her actions, and, in
fact, stands to have her own fairly secure, structured existence radically
altered when her actions are made known. Is it an amatory form of
"sour grapes"—"if I can't have him, no one else can either"? Perhaps,
but this seems too simplistic a motive for her obsessed "stalking" of her
ex-lover and his latest conquest and her eventual destruction of the
man. Her paranoid behavior is never satisfactorily explained and her
motives not wholly clear; whatever they may be, Grau's strength in
this novel is her totally convincing method of presenting a character in
the midst of a struggle with self-destructive tendencies, even if her
motivation is less than lucid.

All in all, *The House on Coliseum Street* is, strictly on formal
grounds, more successful as a novel than the earlier work. One could
wish for greater variety in character portrayal, as well as for a missing
sense of inevitability in the characters' behavior resulting from their
necessary resolutions of forces governing their existence. As it is, the
reader almost, but not quite, gets the uncomfortable feeling that there
should be more, just a bit more at the novel's end, to help put Joan's
actions and disturbed state into perspective. The consequence of the
lack of such needed touches is the sense that the book is contrived and
melodramatic, charges leveled against the work by some of its initial

reviewers (though ironically it has also been called a "novel of manners").[6] It is not the characters or their actions which are in themselves melodramatic so much as Grau's failure to show convincingly how certain situations combined with a certain temperament result in a disturbed individual. Joan may believe that "I wanted none of the things that have happened. . . . They just came along. I didn't intend them. Time and things like a river, passing. . . . Things will go on happening when I am dead. Pass around me and over me and go on" (231). But the fact remains that the reader has to be persuaded of this as well, and mere assertion by the protagonist is not sufficient to make of the novel a wholly satisfying work of fiction.

CHAPTER 4

The Keepers of the House

*T*HE *Keepers of the House*, published in 1964, is by all odds Grau's most ambitious—and in some respects most successful—novel to date. Reviews of the book were adulatory and enthusiastic, it was a selection of both the Literary Guild and the Book-of-the-Month Club, it was cut by about a third and published as a condensed book in the *Ladies Home Journal* (January–February, 1964), and it, like most of Grau's books, went into successive paperback printings. Other writers such as Lillian Smith and Mary Ellen Chase praised the book's "prophetic" quality and its deep sense of moral integrity, citing in particular its violent excitement and Grau's sheer storytelling skill. Grau's earlier work had been respectfully received, but this novel immediately caught the sense of the American reading public by virtue of its overwhelming sense of place, of Grau's ability to create a world in which the reader can believe and which, at the novel's end, he regrets leaving. Her writing had never been more sensuously vibrant with the rhythms of life in the South, and the tension between whites and blacks in that South had rarely escaped the stereotypical caricaturing so often provided as the "true" South. In all respects, it was a major piece of work, with Grau immediately, though in retrospect misleadingly, compared by various critics to the likes of Faulkner. And although major works by such other novelists as Saul Bellow *(Herzog)* and Louis Auchincloss *(The Rector of Justin)* were also published that year, it was *The Keepers of the House* that was awarded the Pulitzer Prize for fiction.

I *Creating a Myth*

There are, to be sure, aspects of the book that immediately led some readers to seek parallels with Faulkner and others, not the least being the fact that Grau in this novel not only creates an entire mythical society, a state not quite corresponding to any of the existing Southern states, but even more establishes a credible dynasty, a family whose successive generations rise and fall and whose overpowering sense of their destiny suggests most immediately the Sutpen clan in *Absalom, Absalom!* But Grau is not a Faulkner, and though such parallels exist, her work can stand by itself simply as a beautifully realized and executed work in which her lyrical power as a writer has almost perfect control and development. It is not an imitation of Faulkner, despite such parallels; but it is a work with brilliant characterization, thorough awareness of pacing and detail, and—compared to Grau's earlier works—more carefully worked-out plotting. Grau calls the book her "most ambitious"[1] and also acknowledges that the novel "has almost exactly" her own family background, with "Howland," the name of the family whose dynastic evolution is at the heart of the novel, not only based on but also with the same surname as her grandfather.[2]

The setting of the novel, as mentioned, is mythical, a deliberate effort to transcend any particular locale or culture in the South— unlike, once again, Faulkner's Yoknapatawpha County. Since Southerners "love to litigate," Grau says she "very carefully went through the novel and scrambled my geography. It's no one place. It's a bit of everything. For that same reason, I went very carefully through the Atlas and checked the names of every county and town in the Southern states against my counties and towns."[3] The most detailed study of the geography of the novel[4] reaches a similar conclusion, that the locale is so deliberately obscured that none of the Southern states exactly fits Grau's descriptions, which Grau, concurring, said was "an attempt to broaden the canvas."[5]

If the setting of the novel is deliberately intended to avoid specific parallels, the moral thrust of the work is not. Not surprisingly, this is the aspect of the novel that came in for strongest praise in the reviews and critiques that appeared shortly after its publication. As the plot summary will show, the crux of the potentially controversial feature of the book is the marriage of a wealthy white widower to his black housekeeper, and the subsequent chaos resulting from the past intruding upon the present. The book is not primarily about racial relations per se, as Grau has commented on various occasions, but miscegenation is most definitely a part of it. Although many works touching on interracial mating have appeared over the years, both before and since *The Keepers of the House* was published and by both southerners and others, such as Sinclair Lewis' *Kingsblood Royal* and Robert Penn Warren's *Band of Angels*, this remains the novel that is perhaps the most offensive to the traditional Southern thinking about race in that the white and black characters both mate with each other and love each other. As Grau says:

Everyone assumes that [*The Keepers of the House*] is about segregation, which is part of it, but emphatically not about segregation in the sense the James Baldwin plays are. It is segregation as one of the many forms of evil.

The novel is about the whole human plight of how do you cope with evil? Do you fight back? The people are living in the South but they're just people facing the eternal human problem. . . .

I wanted to show the alternation of love and evil, which has always fascinated me. And if there is a moral, it is the self-destructiveness of hatred.[6]

Yet the struggle for racial identity and equality is integral to the manner in which these characters interact, and it is race that remains the shibboleth of Southern justice.

Grau had used the Southern black previously in her fiction, particularly in her short stories, and on a number of occasions she and her family received "barrages" of threatening phone calls "from white Southerners who did not like her sympathy for the Negro."[7] Yet she adamantly denies that she was attempting to write social criticism; her chief aim in the novel was to tell a story, in this case the story of the "evil that good men do." The "color problem," she maintains, is a part of the larger problem of good and evil in mankind, an "aspect of evil."[8] Indeed, this can be seen in the concluding pages of *The Keepers of the House*, in which both the staunchly segregationist and the antisegregationist perspectives are equally rejected as insufficient means of resolving the larger manifestation of evil of which racial prejudice is a part.

It is, moreover, evil in its most subversive and insidious forms that seems to be at the heart of the novel, for the bitter racial fight serves primarily to bring antagonists into the open at the novel's end, when all the dynastic manipulations culminate. The bulk of the novel is about race only tangentially, only in the ways in which interracial mating and servant-master relationships continue year after year with little concern for community outrage or turmoil. The past, as in other works concerned with the effects of dynastic manipulation, constantly impinges upon the various forms of the "present" offered in the novel; this is particularly so regarding the human qualities developed generation after generation in the Howland clan, traits finally coming to fruition when chaos erupts all around the Howland home. It is, in a word, the archetypal conflict of the frontier values of the past coming into conflict with the more urban—and urbane—values of today, and the ability of these more traditional concepts not only to stand, but even more—to use a Faulknerian term—to endure.

II *Plot*

The "house" that is "kept" in this novel was originally a structure built by the first (of a line of six similarly named patriarchs) William Howland, a Tennessean who settled in the area following the Battle of New Orleans in 1815. Each successive Howland has both "kept" and added to the "house," both in its literal sense and in the meaning of the larger family community. The last of the sequence, a rugged, long-lived individualist combining rustic simplicity and business genius, is a wealthy but untamed child of the frontier who stands out as one of Grau's most believable and successful characterizations. This William Howland was married twice, the first time to a somewhat ethereal young woman whose frail daughter, Abigail, married an even more insubstantial Englishman; the most important aspect of his first marriage is the birth of a child named Abigail and that of another William, who lived only a year following the death of his mother in childbirth. When Abigail is in college, she marries Gregory Mason, a classmate of hers. Howland, after years of being a presumably ascetic widower, is once again completely alone in the house. To correct this situation, he invites a young woman named Margaret Carmichael, a Negro from the nearby community of New Church, to be his housekeeper, and she becomes the most important figure in Howland's life: first housekeeper, then mistress and mother of three children by him, and then, just before he dies, years later, his wife. And in this we have both the making of Howland's most profound commitment in life as well as the subsequent "scandal" that is to precipitate the near-destruction of the "house" toward the novel's end. The thirty years they spend together, till his death at age seventy-eight, are momentous ones not only for Howland but for the region as a whole. Though the faces of Margaret's children were black and those of Howland's two children by his first marriage were white, all these children were brought up together as equals.

But Margaret knows full well the consequences of her children growing up in the South, even with as high a degree of "white blood" as they carry; consequently, all three—surnamed Carmichael instead of Howland—are raised and educated in the North, and all three, in varying ways, spend their adult years reacting against the burden of color. The oldest, Robert, passes for a white in the North, lives in Washington State, and is married to a white woman. Nina, slightly younger than William's granddaughter, Abigail Mason Howland, has married a black and lives in Philadelphia. And Crissy, the youngest, writes from Paris, "the haven of American Negroes" (242),[9] suggesting that she, "the gentlest and the nicest of Margaret's children" (242), had accepted her racial identity in a way neither of her siblings had in their self-conscious rejection of blackness and segregation (Robert) or self-conscious debasement in calling attention to her status (Nina).

The narrator of the novel is Abigail Mason Howland, William's granddaughter, who returns to her home in the South at the age of eight, knowing that that is where she belongs; if her British father's returning to England in 1939 (142) can be taken as the time when she and her mother returned to Madison City, a valid assumption, then Abigail was born in 1931 and is in her forties during the climactic closing section of the novel.

In her narration, Abigail provides historical perspective in the lives of her grandfather and others in an omniscient manner that suggests an attempt to find out the meaning of history as this has led several generations of Howlands to merge imperceptibly and totally with their region; only Abigail possesses the necessary perspective by which the various interrelationships can be seen to make sense, even though in so doing she ceases being an individual character and assumes the godlike role of omniscient narrator for most of the novel. In the sections specifically concerned with the "now," with Abigail's own growing-up from adolescent to college student to wife and mother, she seems to know considerably less than she did in the earlier sections of the book, limited as she is to events concerned only with her immediate family.

And indisputably a major part of that maturation process is Abigail's unquestioning acceptance of Southern mores regarding racial relations and biblical justification for racial prejudice. We are told, for example, that she was taught Bible lessons in such a way that "to this day [she was] very good at spotting signs of Negro blood and at reciting the endless lists of genealogies in the Bible. It's a southern talent, you might say" (143). Combined with this is a sense of *noblesse oblige* in which the dominant white society knows the security of their position to such a degree that even potentially scandalous activities, such as William

Howland's having a black mistress, cause no undue reaction: "My mother liked Margaret. Maybe because Margaret had everything she hadn't: size and strength and physical endurance. Maybe my mother was so sure of her own position that she couldn't be challenged by her father's Negro mistress. And maybe, too, maybe as simple as this: my mother was a lady and a lady is unfailingly polite and gentle to everyone . . ." (149). Growing up, Abigail and other white children did not play with the black children: "I don't know why. Most times we didn't even see them" (155).

Abigail's mother died when she was sixteen (i.e., 1947) and the year after, when her father returned from England to see her, she was suddenly taken on an extensive vacation to the American West. She then attends college, is nearly expelled but is reinstated because of her grandfather's influence, and then, wholly by accident, is introduced by her grandfather to John Tolliver, the law student who is to become her husband. The Tollivers come from—one might say "run"—Somerset County, the "northernmost county with the darkest, bloodiest past in the state" (194), and John, the family heir-apparent, knows from the outset that he is meant for major political service. She knows matter-of-factly that she will marry John, and he similarly indifferently asks her to do so. Abigail loves her husband, but does not particularly like him. And as his rapid rise to political success continues, she finds herself liking him less and less, primarily because he attempts to be "all things to all men," telling staunch segregationists what they wish to hear about the innate genetic inferiority of blacks and promising blacks what they wish to hear. Abigail and John have three children, two girls and a boy, the same as William and Margaret had had, and during the extensive separations that Abigail and John experience, the children become Abigail's chief reason for existence, particularly after her grandfather dies one wintry day, alone, out in the country slumped over the steering wheel of his truck.

Bit by bit the inexorable culmination of all these forces combines to work on Abigail in such a way that she increasingly questions her relationship with her husband and with all the others who are or who have been an intimate part of her life. When Nina comes South with her black husband (227), Abigail knows instinctively that her outburst of disapproval to Nina and her husband smacks of condemnation. Abigail knows that Nina's returning South is a form of self-pity (228), and that although she—Abigail—may therefore be called a white bigot, she must still tell Nina and her husband that she will not intercede with

Margaret, not even to acknowledge to Margaret that Nina has visited. When Abigail says to Nina, "Margaret didn't ask you to come. Nobody sent for you" (228), she is not only speaking aloud the feelings she knows Margaret has at the moment, she also bravely says what has to be said to Nina to let her know of her cowardly rejection of all that Margaret attempted to inculcate in her. That is, Nina, by deliberately choosing to be a part of the "black" world when every influence and opportunity has been given her to be part of the "white" world, has turned her back on the very values her mother had lived by. Small wonder that neither Margaret nor Abigail wishes to see Nina and her husband, for their match—in the terms used by Abigail and Margaret at the time—is a deliberate rejection of all the upwardly mobile impulses Margaret had tried to develop in Nina.

Abigail, having her own life and world to consider, soon forgets about Nina. But she cannot forget the black world. In town one day, she sees the small black youth who had previously brought a message from Margaret. When the boy shows no sign of recognition, Abigail first refers to him as "the impenetrable African" (232), and then is self-consciously aware of her own attitudes toward blacks: "I had done what most white people around here did—knew a Negro and dealt with him for years, and never found out his name. Never got curious about who he was, and what he was called. As if Negroes didn't need identities . . ." (233). And when Margaret herself dies—evidently a willing death caused by walking into the very baptistry waters where she and William had first met, and on the fourth anniversary of his death—Abigail even further realizes the gulf between her traditional attitudes and those gradually emerging. When she hears from Nina, she coldly replies with words about Margaret's suicide, despite the legal doubt about such motives as self-destruction implies: "Carry that behind your arrogant handsome face. Guilt for being a Negro, guilt for having a suicide for a mother" (236). But a mystical communion of sorts exists between the dead Margaret and the live Abigail, only tentatively suggested in the passages already cited but more forcibly demonstrated in the description of a lonely early-morning drive Abigail makes when she returns home from a day of volunteer visitation at a hospital some miles from home. She is driving rapidly down the deserted highway, knowing full well that even the state troopers are off-duty for several hours, when suddenly her radio—constantly on otherwise—goes silent. And it remains silent as she speeds along the highway till she is within sight of her ancestral home, itself described in a hallucinatory manner: "But of course it was there. Vague and indistinct in the fog, but there, just the way it had been for the last five generations. It looked very very large in this light, and empty. Fog covered the fields beneath it, so that it seemed to float without solid ground, just exactly like those fairy castles in a child's story book" (246). At that very moment the radio goes on, and Abigail wonders and realizes that "there'd been a message of some sort. Something had brushed right by [her]—for good or evil [she] didn't know. Because [she] hadn't understood" (247). But the message, if such it is, does become clearer as time goes on, and it amounts to a renewed sense of place, of commitment to the house that she and the others had "kept" for so long, because "when you live in a place you've always lived in . . . you get to see things not only in space but in time too" (247). She thus realizes that she alone must preserve the best of the past, the house and all it stands for, not to rely on others to do so. The fifteen years she has been married are, she realizes, at an end because she and her husband have increasingly grown polarized over the racial issue, with John more and more soliciting the help of the Klan and the White Citizens' Councils for aid in getting reelected.

Then chaos erupts. A photostat of the marriage license between her grandfather and Margaret Carmichael is published in a major newspaper; Robert, Margaret's militant son, comes to visit, accompanied by a horde of reporters and photographers, and the visit clearly shows the depth of the anger and guilt he feels not only at having deserted his mother, but also in being the instrument of calling attention to the truth about the Howland family's racial "purity." Abigail, realizing that everything is collapsing around her, threatens Robert with even greater vengeance than he is wreaking then, because she knows full well the extent of his self-destructive guilt over his "blackness," even though he is married to a white woman.

Abigail's husband, ever the aggressively opportunistic politician, comes to the house to say in essence that he is choosing his career over his family. And for the first time Abigail is alone, aside from her children: "All my life I had been trained to depend on men, now when I needed them they were gone" (275). Her need, simply stated, is for assistance in saving herself and her children, as well as her ancestral home: a mob of angry white men have gathered near the entrance to the farm, intent on avenging themselves on what is the Howland "betrayal" of their racial ethos. They first shoot the cattle, then come closer to set fire to the barn. As they do so, Abigail and Oliver, the faithful old black servant who had been in the family for decades, set fire to the vigilantes' cars. Finally the state police arrive, deliberately delayed because they sympathize with the barn-burners and were reluctant to intercede until the vigilantes' own property was afire.

The epilogue to the novel shows Abigail filing for divorce from John and setting her financial affairs in order. She had never previously realized the extent to which the Howlands own the entire county, especially Madison City. So at what is alleged to be a shower for a bride but is in reality a public viewing of the Abigail Howland Tolliver who has dared to fight fire with fire, she announces that she is deliberately closing first the hotel, then the slaughter house and packing plant and ice-cream factory and lumber business—in short, everything that has brought the town from its rural slumber decades earlier and the loss of which will force the town back into its earlier inertia: "You watch. This town's going to shrivel and shrink back to its real size. . . . It wasn't Will Howland you burned down, it was your own house" (306). Even here, Abigail is intent upon demonstrating how she, as the last "keeper of the house," also helps those who were responsible, even passively, for the attack realize that they have simply done far more damage to their own well-being than they have to hers. The novel is now at its end, and Abigail, weeping, first calls Robert in Seattle to remind him that she is also going to bring his "house" down, and then falls to the floor in a fetal position, huddling against the "cold unyielding boards" of the "house" she has kept in the independent spirit of her grandfather and her stepmother.

III   *The Mythic Quality of the Characters*

The sheer scale of this novel, resulting from Grau's sense of the mythic, her awareness of the intense patterns of meaning cohesively holding all the other elements of the book together, has elicited comparisons between the work and Greek tragedy.[10] This is no idle comparison, for it is the scale and stature of the Howland line which perseveres, despite the loss of individual members of the dynasty, and which maintains its integrity by remaining in the same family home generation after generation. In this sense the book's title has an intentional ambiguity, for the "house" as both residents and as lineage continues unbroken. Grau's title comes from Ecclesiastes 12:3-5, also used by T. S. Eliot in *The Waste Land,* and is itself a suggestive parallel to the events presented in the novel:

In the day when the keepers of the house shall tremble, and the strong men shall bow themselves, and the grinders cease because they are few, and those that look out of the windows be darkened,

And the doors shall be shut in the streets, when the sound of the grinding is low, and he shall rise up at the voice of the bird, and all the daughters of musick shall be brought low,

Also when they shall be afraid of that which is high, and fears shall be in the way, and the almond tree shall flourish, and the grasshopper shall be a burden, and desire shall fail: because man goeth to his long home, and the mourners go about the streets.

The inevitability suggested by this passage, with the "long home" implying one's grave, fully fits the life and times of William Howland the last; Margaret Carmichael, his second wife; and Abigail Mason Howland, his granddaughter. For these are, in their different ways, among the strongest characters in all of Grau's fiction. The relationship each has to the physical house is also great, because each becomes a part of the house and works to preserve it from whatever form of attack occurs.

The narrator of the novel, Abigail, begins with the words, "I want to tell you the story of my grandfather, and Margaret Carmichael, and me" (9). Just as each generation had a William Howland, so each successively named head of the house put his distinctive mark on the place in such a manner as to preserve it from attack and to strengthen it against decay. It can well be said that the last William Howland "owned" the entire community, as well as the surrounding countryside. But not until the "house" is attacked is there any reason for this either to be known or for the power implicit in such total control to be exercised. The last William Howland had virtually single-handedly created the wealth enjoyed by Madison City, with almost all industries and other forms of employment dependent upon his good graces. Such a description as the foregoing makes him seem like a "benevolent patriarch" akin to nineteenth-century capitalist tycoons; there is, however, a qualitative difference, and that is that Howland unostentatiously uses the accumulated wealth and power not to influence public opinion or to build monuments to himself, but only to enhance the general economy and, as needed, to benefit his own, as when Abigail has to be readmitted into college by virtue of her grandfather's influence. The label "rugged individualist," were it not used so often in the pejorative sense, would perhaps more appropriately apply.

The first William Howland, a Tennessean, moved into the geo-

graphic area that became Madison City in 1815. From the inception
of the line, a highly individualistic following of personal convictions
over public opinion characterized the Howlands; the second in the line,
for example, married a Roman Catholic, a highly radical and even
subversive thing to do at the time in an area wholly Baptist and Methodist. And when the William Howland who serves as the novel's protagonist was widowed, leaving a daughter to raise by himself, he quietly continues following his own leaning, totally unconcerned for
gossipy talk about a possible mistress and his alleged need for a new
wife. As his daughter, also named Abigail, prepares for her wedding,
Howland wrestles with unusual, recurring impulses: "Way down in the
pit of his stomach there was a soft tugging, as if he were straining
toward the earth" (47–48). As the house fills up for his daughter's wedding, he finds himself in the way, so he escapes to the old unused mill,
down on the creek. And when he is again alone, with all the wedding
guests scattered to the towns from which they came, he sets about
doing the outside chores that had accumulated, restless until he realizes
what he will do. It is then that he prepares for the major event in his
adult life, the archetypal journey into the wilderness, a journey paralleled in numerous other works concerned with the erosion of the frontier. He goes—completely alone, of course—into the deep swamp and
marsh country, far beyond the woods known to him since childhood,
into virtually uncharted country where only the occasional moonshiner
ventures. At first he plans merely to play a trick on some moonshiners
by leaving them a note saying that he had been there, but the further
out he goes into the uncharted swamp, the more he senses anew the
vitality of youth. His careful manner of marking his way, of sampling
water and plant life, of observing and studying everything coming
within his view, and of methodically adapting to and therefore overcoming the forces he encounters in the swamp, enable him to take on
a larger-than-human stature. For example, when a cloud of biting
gnats attacks him, he does the only commonsensical thing he can in the
circumstances: strip off his clothing, cover himself with thick mud, and
put his clothes on top of the mud. He dispatches a rattler's attack with
the same cool ease, and continues on his journey, knowing only in a
general way that he is near a community named New Church, an isolated area occupied only by a few Freejack Negroes. These were slaves
who had fought with Andrew Jackson at the Battle of New Orleans
and who had received their freedom for loyal service; keeping themselves aloof and apart from other blacks and mixing with various Indi-

ans or whites as the generations passed, the few remaining Freejacks were themselves almost mythical beings because of the lore that had grown up concerning them.

And while Howland fights his way back to familiar terrain, near New Church, he first sights the eighteen-year-old Margaret Carmichael, silently washing clothes by hand near what was once a baptistry. At this point he is forty-eight years of age; in a sense, he is just now beginning to live, for all his previous adult life has been spent in caring for his family, both those who had died and the daughter that remained. Even at the wedding, Howland suddenly realizes that although white men say all black men looked alike, "to him now, niggers looked different" (54). Hence when he finds Margaret, he spontaneously and without hesitation asks her to come to live with him. Not a paragon of virtue, William Howland is simply a man large enough in stature to do as he senses is right without concern for possible reaction from others. In a totally unself-conscious way, he deliberately changes the course of the dynasty's future.

Margaret—part black, part white, tall, regal, proud—not only learns the ways of the Howland home, but soon becomes indispensable. As Howland's granddaughter puts it: "Living with him, she lived with us all, all the Howlands, and her life got mixed up with ours. Her face was black and ours were white, but we were together anyhow. Her life and his. And ours (78). Her adaptability and stoical acceptance of the inevitable are characteristics which appear in this woman throughout the novel: "And it be right strange, she told herself silently, the way things come in their seasons. The way they appear and go each year at the same time, without ever a mistake. . . . And the way people come. And me, I am here now, but I won't be next year" (113). In her affinity to the natural order, Margaret is reminiscent of the echoes of Ecclesiastes (3:1–8), with its sense of the natural inevitability of the world and its processes, in the novel's title.

A perfect example of the "earth mother," Margaret, despite her size, seems to fold herself into the earth as she sits "perched, suspended on the very crust" (117). Howland, however, realizes how much she changes in the days after her arrival, particularly in the alteration from sitting childlike on the ground contrasted with her movements when she walks, "a primitive walk, effortless, unassuming, unconscious, old as the earth under her feet" (129).

A lengthy flashback section describes Margaret's own growing-up, with all the accompanying awareness of human mortality (when her

mother dies) and mutability (at the realization that though she may be
at New Church one moment, she may well be someplace entirely
unexpected the year later), and then, from her perspective, describes
her meeting with Howland, for whom she pulls up stakes as easily as
if she had only been at New Church for minutes instead of for her
entire adult life. It is as if she had been awaiting just such a turn of
events in her life, being recognized by a white man (she had endlessly
thought about her own white father) and then following him to
become a part of his life. The same passive, acquiescent acceptance of
life is stoically expressed by her grandfather when she tells him of her
plans to leave: "Nothing for you to do here. . . . You got to be moving
on" (120). And when Howland dies, leaving Margaret, she adjusts once
again, after thirty years of living at the Howland homestead, as quickly
as she did when first she went to live with Will. She moves out at once,
back to the dilapidated shacks near the old baptistry, where she lives
for four years—to the day—following Will's death.

Will's granddaughter, Abigail, is by far the most important of the
three "keepers," and also one of the strongest, most memorable women
in recent American fiction. From childhood on she had been raised
with traditional Southern teaching regarding both race and religion.
Abigail too echoes passages from Ecclesiastes (1:6, 3:1–8) when she first
hears that her mother has died—"Something about the wind blowing
over the grass and the seasons of things, but I couldn't quite remember
it" (171–72). Her childhood and adolescence are spent going through
the normal rituals of discovering alcohol and sex, of fast driving and
the vast array of attitudes toward traditional issues, and only slowly
does she learn the meaning of wisdom. For example, she once taunts
her grandfather about taking a taxi all the way from her college to the
homestead, observing that since he would not arrive till after midnight,
he must miss Margaret, saying all this as a joke. His eyes go cold as she
speaks, and a hasty apology leads him only to say, "You're a child, and
like your mother you have very little sense" (192). Speaking the unnecessary, she finds, can be cruel.

Her marriage to John Tolliver seems, from the reader's perspective,
less than ideal; though Abigail does not like her husband, she does love
him. And as he aggressively builds a political power-base by appealing
to the racial prejudice and ignorance of the voters and by linking himself to the White Citizens' Councils and the Klan, she is more and more
alienated from him. It is necessary for her to be totally independent,
since her husband is gone so much of the time, so she quickly assumes

total charge of the family homestead, where life goes on contentedly until Margaret's son Robert intrudes upon her comfortable life after Margaret's alleged suicide. After this, life is never again simple or comfortable. Abigail gradually develops a kind of inner sight, first experienced with the silence of the car radio as she drove home early one morning. As she says,

It's like this, when you live in a place you've always lived in, where your family has always lived. You get to see things not only in space but in time too. . . . That's the way it is with me. I see them as they were. I see them all around in time. And this is bad. Because it makes you think you know a place. Because it makes you think you know the people in it. (248–49).

But she clearly does not know people in a particular place, because she admits that she does not really know her husband of fifteen years when he walks out upon the newspaper publication of her grandfather and Margaret's wedding certificate (258). She says, "That's all. I loved him once, but I don't seem to any more, because I'm not sorry to see him go" (273).

Finally, Abigail's tenacity and courage are well illustrated when the gang of hoodlums attempts to burn down the Howland home. Her daughter, Abby, is at first frightened of the possibility of having the home burn down with them in it, but Abigail soothes her by telling of an account of one of their ancestors, the mother of a girl killed by a mob of bandits, who laughed with glee when the bandits were caught and hanged, as if to say that the family's heritage has always been one of violence and that there was no running away from the threat of violence and death (279).

Abigail's total victory over the gang of barn-burners leads to her consequent victory over the entire community. For in the best tradition of the Greek tragedies with which the book has been compared, Abigail enacts vengeance against all those who have threatened her and her home. In even this she is acting responsibly as a "keeper" of the house, for the "house" of Madison City would be and is nothing without the influx of Howland money from her and her grandfather. She and her family would not be affected adversely by her decision to withdraw funds from the family businesses, though all others in the community would suffer her wrath. And in rejecting the easy answers of both the segregationists (identified with her ex-husband) and the various positions of Margaret's children, she is in effect saying, "A plague on both your houses!" once again suggesting—by inference—that she intends to remain as "keeper" of the Howland house as long as she can, and that her children will continue in the same tradition.

All three of these major figures are strong, vigorous, unpretentious characters, not easily swayed, not cowardly, not prone to blame others when circumstances demand of them total loyalty to the "house of Howland." The Howlands are indeed a dynasty, but one based not on mere family continuity so much as on the awareness that what they must preserve is both worth preserving and at the same time strong enough to endure any attacks upon it. William Howland may pass on, and so may Margaret; and when Abigail herself departs, then young Abby will no doubt continue, since there are no more William Howlands. In the end the "keepers of the house" will still prevail.

IV   Critical Evaluation

As already suggested, the parallel between this novel and such grand-scale literary sources as Greek tragedy has been made; whether such parallels exist or not is open to question, but the fact that they were made suggests that the book's initial impact led critics to try to find hyperbolic forms of praise for the work. Grau's accomplishment in the novel is not diminished by pointing out the obvious, that her desire to answer the question "How do you cope with evil?"—the same "eternal human problem" found in almost all literature, Greeks down to our day—is a question requiring particularly dramatic answers when set in the transitional South. All the major characters in the book attempt to cope with the question of evil, each responding to and handling the problem in his or her own way. Yet, as Grau astutely pointed out in an interview, "All of them make the same mistake—that love will somehow or other surmount evil. I wanted to show the alternation of love and evil, which has always fascinated me. And if there is a moral, it is the self-destructiveness of hatred."[11] Indeed, as one critic pointed out, those in Madison City who hate in the most overt manner "continue to exterminate themselves. The novel demonstrates that their only liberty is lamentation."[12] And "lamentation" offers yet another Old Testament parallel to Grau's novel, since the net effect of Abigail's ruining the city economically is the same as if some modern "plague of locusts" had wiped out an agrarian community.

Grau evidently intended to create something of just such a mythical nature in this novel, for in commenting, as quoted earlier, that she was "attempting to broaden" her "canvas," she added that she had hoped "to make the meaning of the story something more than the story itself."[13] And she has also commented, regarding this novel, that

when you are writing novels you are always aware of the symbolic meaning of your characters' actions. You have to be; otherwise, you never get off the level of just telling a story. You want to tell a story that has implications, and the implications could be symbols. . . . I wanted to look at the way good and evil affect the lives of people who live in the center. And in this sense, because good and evil are abstract symbolic notions, the story has a symbolic interpretation.[14]

It is, then, the sheer scale of this novel that contrasts both with Grau's earlier work and with the work of much other recent "Southern" fiction. The repeated allusions to Old Testament parallels and sources found both in the novel itself and in various critical comments support one's view that it is William Howland's patriarchal qualities, as the final larger-than-life person of that name in the Howland lineage, that dominates the book. The passage from Ecclesiastes used as the epigraph to the novel and the source of the title refers to those who "shall be afraid of that which is high," which could be taken to refer to Howland; as dominant resident of the area in both personality and financial influence, he is clearly one who strikes fear in the hearts of others when he is crossed, just as his granddaughter's courageous routing of the mob at the novel's end suggests that she has inherited the same quality.

Grau insists that the color problems in this novel are "just aspects of evil. They are not so important in themselves, but as representatives of a larger problem."[15] She is undoubtedly correct in pointing out the manner in which the novel confronts this "larger problem" of evil; yet the same "problem" is to be found in all of her fiction, because of both her conscious intent and the inescapable conclusions reached by a reader. This novel, however, succeeds in ways in which none of the rest of her long fiction succeeds, and to answer the question of why this is so requires our being aware of the way in which the book grew out of her entire experience—family and region, events of the past century as well as those of the more recent present, the persistence with which such ideas as miscegenation refuse to die in the Deep South, and the entire Judeo-Christian tradition of good overcoming the pervasive evil lurking in all of us.

Yet even this explains only the conscious substance of the novel. Perhaps ultimately the book's success is due to Grau's having surpassed anything she had done previously or since, not just in moral outrage, but on more formal levels simply as an example of the craft of fiction. For noble though Grau's intent may be in *The Keepers of the House*, the novel would be little more than a fictional tract for brotherhood were it not for her demonstrably superior handling of character and plot in this work, as well as her profoundly moving sense of the importance of certain values in the lives of these characters.

Neither of her subsequent novels has the same narrative power, depth of characterization, resolution of the various plot-strands at the work's denouement, or symbolic tying-together all of these into a unified, convincing, and total work of fiction. All of this does not suggest that Grau has not continued to try to equal this, her "most ambitious" novel, only that, in the jargon of the entertainment industry, *The Keepers of the House* was a "tough act to follow." Whatever Grau's status as a novelist may ultimately be, it will surely be *The Keepers of the House* that is cited as her best work.

CHAPTER 5

The Condor Passes

GRAU'S fourth novel, *The Condor Passes*, appeared in 1971 to a mixed but generally hostile reception. Critics commented unfavorably on many features of the book, ranging from her repeating the form of her previous novel, to her unfortunate use of the condor as a symbol that simply does not work, to her use of repulsive characters, and, most often, to her evident attempt to capitalize on the success of Mario Puzo's *The Godfather*, published in 1969. In general, critics felt that she had suffered a lapse in a notable literary career and that she was capable of much more than she had demonstrated in *The Condor Passes*. Still, this book sold more than all of her other books combined and it was chosen as a selection by the Book-of-the-Month Club; but these facts do not diminish the criticisms which, if sustainable, would suggest that Grau's earlier successes were all she was capable of. In retrospect, one can see the validity of some of the criticisms, especially that regarding the symbol of the condor. But there are other aspects of the novel which appear to make it seem considerably more consistent with Grau's career, both earlier and subsequent, than one would conclude from the excessive condemnation given it by its initial critics in the press.

I *Parallels with* The Godfather

First and perhaps most important is its parallels with Puzo's book. Any work on the same subject would have had a difficult time matching Puzo's blockbuster epic about Mafia families in New York, even though it had far more than its share of melodrama, one-dimensional characters, gratuitous sex and violence, and other titillating appeals to a bourgeois readership's interest in renegade capitalists from an ethnic subculture; one can see quite easily why a number of Italian-American organizations protested the book's seeming indictment of all Italians in the country. But Grau's book has little in common with Puzo's other

than that both deal with the world of crime, and, therefore, that both
contain some of the same types of incidents.

One must point out, however, that Grau had her book substantially
completed before Puzo's appeared in 1969, and that as a result of these
similarities, she made material changes before hers was finally published two years later. In reply to a question about *The Condor Passes*
not reflecting her own background or the world she had personally
experienced, she observed, in 1969:

> It is more of a no-background novel than a heavy-background novel, like *The
> Keepers of the House*. It takes place roughly on the Florida Gulf coast. The
> setting, though, is less than the people. You can't live in New Orleans and not
> know many Italian families who've made it big with a start as rumrunners.
> After reading *The Godfather* by Mario Puzo, I wondered if I couldn't change
> things around a little, but I'd gotten too far into my own novel. . . . It's a little
> infuriating to find the parallel.[1]

Even in this statement, however, it is obvious that her novel as published had undergone considerable metamorphosis from its initial versions. For one thing, the emphasis on an Italian family is completely
gone, and the setting, for another, is more closely related to the area
south of New Orleans—roughly the area used as setting in *The Hard
Blue Sky*—than it is to the Florida Gulf. Indeed, the parallels with *The
Hard Blue Sky* include, in addition to setting, the use of family names
also used in the earlier novel. Oliver's wife, Stephanie D'Alphonso, is
evidently from the same family as Inky D'Alphonso, caretaker of the
boat in *The Hard Blue Sky;* and when Robert, to check on the causes
of the Old Man's boats being burned during Prohibition, hires a
shrimpboat to take him to the area where the fires occurred, he hires
one operated by a man named Landry, the same family name used by
Annie Landry in the earlier novel. While direct connections are omit-
ted, there seems no valid reason for the similarity of names except for
continuity between novels.

Hence Grau's novel, though admittedly a flawed production, has little in common with Puzo's melodramatic glimpses into the New York
crime world; both as originally conceived and as subsequently published, Grau's is less about the world of crime than it is about the interplay of two of her favorite themes, love and money. For, as she has
observed in a later interview, *The Condor Passes*

is not the longest of my works, but it's the most complex. I've tried to do something different from what I had done before. Until now, I've dealt with fairly primitive people. The characters in *Condor* are no longer concerned merely with survival. They have an awful lot of money, and they have problems of personal identity, of love, and the problems are more evident as a result of the money, because life always becomes more complicated when you remove the immediate economic push.

Love and money are two themes which I have always found fascinating . . . the effect of one on the other, and in this book, I tried to explore the possibilities. . . . And I think the book is more ambitious than my others, and a lot less Southern.[2]

Although the exploration of these two themes does not require the use of the world of crime, it nonetheless is true that writers and audiences alike find the shadowy underworld, especially the oft-told story of how respectable fortunes originated in devious and illicit enterprises, as fascinating today as when the muckrakers exposed nineteenth-century robber-baron capitalists. Grau's book could have concerned any nonagenarian millionaire, not merely one whose start came, as in *The Condor Passes*, with hustling for money while still in his teens, who progressed to greater crimes, who flourished—as did so many others, respectable and scoundrel alike—during Prohibition, and who in his dotage reflects upon his career and wasted opportunities. Hence to cite parallels with *The Godfather* or any other novel explicitly about crime is completely misleading, since crime is merely Grau's "hook" upon which she can explore her characters' experiences with love and money.

II *Plot and Setting*

The Condor Passes tells the story of Thomas Henry Oliver, who at age ninety-five has had a full if not emotionally rich life, and who dies after the reader has had a chance to find out the reasons for his wealth and his family's incapacity to love. Always called either by his last name alone, even by his mother when he was a boy, or "The Old Man," as a result of having gone almost completely bald by age thirty, Oliver has led a varied life in his struggle to survive. Born in 1870, he lived as a boy with his impoverished mother in a river town in Ohio where, as a kind of "Huckleberry Finn" youth, he saw men drag the river for a drowned man. Muscular even at age thirteen, he left home

then and survived first as pickpocket, then burglar, pimp (at age fifteen), sailor, smuggler, and gun-runner, before, at age thirty, landing
near New Orleans and jumping ship when smallpox is discovered on
board. In his travels around the world he had seen condors in Chile
and Peru, condors which were to return later in his life as the name of
his yacht and as a myth he cannot forget. In New Orleans he becomes
co-owner of a combination bar and whorehouse, with Alonzo Manzini
his partner. Even at this time Oliver has elaborate plans for his life,
including perfect control over his body. He expands his holdings to
include gambling operations and he meets Maurice Lamotta, whom he
puts through school to prepare for a career as Oliver's financial man-
ager and manipulator. Oliver brings his mother to New Orleans and
sets her up in a fine house; since he has not seen her in over twenty
years, there is no deep affection when she comes and no profound grief
when she dies a couple of years later.

Oliver does, however, find Stephanie D'Alphonso, seventeen-year-
old student at Newcomb College (which Grau attended), appealing
enough to marry. And in 1912, at the age of forty-two, Oliver marries
this young woman. In eleven years of marriage, his wife bears five
children, only two of whom live, his daughters Anna and Margaret;
during the last birth, Stephanie dies. During World War I, Oliver
becomes even richer when a shirt factory he had bought contracts to
make uniforms for the army; he subsequently makes his fortune in
bootlegging and liquor-running during Prohibition. He meets Robert
Caillet, a bright Cajun youth who works for him; Caillet in turn is
groomed as a proxy "son," and in time Robert marries Oliver's daughter Anna. The marriage is an unfortunate one because of Robert's
promiscuity, which eventually reaches even to the level of his finding
satisfaction only with very young virgins. Robert and Anna's only
child, Anthony, is dying from leukemia; and during World War II,
when his father is overseas and his mother keeps him a virtual prisoner,
Anthony slips off in a small boat into the gulf, never again to be seen.
Oliver's other daughter, Margaret, increasingly runs the varied Oliver
businesses, after Robert proves incapable of doing so; herself promiscuous and married several times, Margaret becomes by default the son
Oliver had always hoped for. Her own son, Joshua, becomes a priest,
thus effectively ending the Oliver family line.

By virtue of Oliver's longevity, the novel encompasses a wide spectrum in both time and space. His own travels had taken him throughout the world, and Grau's descriptions of these travels, especially his

sojourn in South America where he first sights the condor, are generally effective. After coming to New Orleans, most of Oliver's remaining adult life is spent there, with his dotage in his palatial home some two hundred miles from New Orleans. The time covered by the novel ranges from the frontier Ohio River life of the 1870s he experienced as a boy, through New Orleans' most celebrated days at the turn of the century and after, through two world wars, and down to his death in 1965. One would be tempted to call such a long life a rich one as well, but such was not the case with Oliver. For his entire life had been spent in financial manipulation and control of other people, not in wise emotional investment.

III   *Characters*

A   *Oliver*

All the major characters in the novel other than Oliver—his two daughters, Robert, and Stanley, a black man who cares for Oliver for over twenty years—are seen only as their lives are affected by Oliver. Oliver's entire existence has been spent in a deliberate climb upward. Even as a teenager, completely on his own, Oliver knows the inexorable path his life will follow. At age thirteen he makes a "deal with God" (41)[3] for the life he has chosen as a means of escaping the terrible poverty he and his mother endure, and as he succeeds in making money, he sends it back to his mother to invest in land. When he jumps ship near New Orleans, he is caught in a whirlpool which he escapes by assuming a "fetus-like" position (60), suggesting, of course, that at this time he—like other Grau protagonists—is being reborn into a new existence different from his previous one. And as he becomes a power in New Orleans, he makes "abstract, detailed plans for the rest of his life. He decided what he must do in each succeeding year, in his personal life, in his business. He had schedules for both, and he intended to keep them" (80). Among the items on his schedule, for example, is getting married when he reaches the age of forty-five (86), a plan he has to alter when his mother dies prematurely (94).

Oliver's subsequent life is spent in acquiring more and more wealth and, we must assume, in developing somewhat the same avaricious tendencies in his two young daughters following their mother's death. While still in his fifties he is considered an old man (112), and his first heart attack occurs when his daughters are barely in their twenties,

and he is sixty-five. Hence he cannot but be aware of his own mortality
and the effect his death would have on his empire; thus, in selecting
Robert, then twenty-one, immediately after his wife dies, Oliver
attempts to insure the continuity of the world he has built up. Oliver
intends that Robert marry his daughter Anna as a means of continuing
the dynasty, so in the first years he employs Robert, Oliver even goes
so far as to interfere with the young man's love affairs in order to
groom him to be Anna's husband (124–26), for Oliver believes that
there is "Nothing that hasn't got a price" (134–35). Therefore, "buy-
ing" a husband for his older daughter seems appropriate.

The degree to which this suggests that Oliver believes that even one's
emotional and marital lives are subordinate to the craving for money
cannot be overestimated, for throughout his life Oliver has maintained
a careful distinction between the demands of his duty as a husband
and father and the economic implications of being a procurer and
manipulator. For example, when Oliver first observes Robert's potential and asks him to come in with him, he, Oliver, has just lost a wife
and gone to a particularly repulsive whore for physical comfort (106–
7). When Robert attempts to act independently of the Old Man's
wishes, Oliver solves the problem of handling Robert and Anna by a
four-month trip to the West, which concludes with Robert's being
engaged to Anna. Again, Oliver has found the "price" needed to purchase something, in this case a son-in-law. And on the very night that
Anna and Robert begin their married life together, Oliver, too, goes to
bed with a woman, one equally as conservative and conventional as
the wife Robert now has. Ironically, Margaret, Oliver's other daughter,
also loses her virginity the same night as Anna, completing the family's
sexual "togetherness." But Oliver finds not only that he is impotent that
night, but even more that the end of lust has set him "free" from the
bondage of his body (210–11). From then till the end of his life, Oliver
is content with living quietly, usually near his daughters, until the day
he decides to have Stanley drive him to visit all the old places he had
known in New Orleans. Changed though the places are in which he
had lived and operated as a youth, the trip is evidently a means of
Oliver's seeing his entire life in perspective, or, as Stanley puts it (384),
as a form of the Old Man's own funeral procession.

Equally obvious at the time that Oliver dies is the fact that the
"dynasty" will soon cease to be, for Anna and Robert's only child has
died and Margaret's is a priest. Anna and Robert are totally alienated
from each other, primarily because Robert has proven to be an
extremely poor choice, not just as a son-in-law but even more as a

human being, since his entire existence is spent with extremely young girls. Among the Old Man's last decisions is eliminating Robert from the control and operations of the financial holdings of the Oliver family, with the two daughters thereafter determining all policy. But Robert's failure as a "son" only serves to emphasize the fact that all that has been built up so laboriously and carefully will itself someday, not too far into the future, also cease being a part of the family. Hence Oliver's death, though anticipated because of his advanced age and his history of heart attacks, serves also to suggest that the consequence of a loveless existence is itself a loveless and pathetic future to look toward. Money may indeed have bought for Oliver everything he wanted, but it could not purchase the kind of love needed to assure that his "success" would continue beyond his death, no matter how vivid his memories of youthful poverty.

Ironically, it may well be this moral emptiness in Oliver that makes him seem so insubstantial to the reader. Whether as a young man on his way up in the world or a successful older man on his way toward death, at no point does Oliver really become as full-bodied a character as one would wish for, since, after all, the novel is more his story than that of anyone else. One may find aspects of his memorable life and career that are individually fascinating, but the man as a whole seems as sterile when one has finished the novel as Oliver's wife seems to him after her death.

One may conclude, therefore, that Oliver's success story is a fluke of a kind, for as an operator outside the law he seems unconvincing, as a capitalist he seems too weak to prosper, as a man establishing his own world of family controls and dynastic succession he seems ineffectual, and as a human being he seems too weak even to espouse his particular variety of selfishness and indifference toward those he presumably loves, as when, because he cannot stand the sight of blood, he leaves his wife during her confinement for each pregnancy. It may well be, then, that the chief failure of execution in this novel is simply Grau's inability to capture completely the character of a man presented unconvincingly as larger than life, for in this one specific effort, Grau's success is considerably less than Puzo's in his novel.

B *Anna*

Anna, by contrast to her father, is so ethereal and romantic that she seems completely insubstantial. We are told that as a child she was obsessed with weddings to the point that she had all her hundreds of

dolls redressed in bridal garb. Deeply religious and devoted to her particular ascetic, otherworldly form of Catholicism, Anna's romantic
nature is fully evidenced by her choosing a wedding gown for herself
modeled after one in an illustration from Scott's *Ivanhoe* (163), the
same source for her expensive "castle" or "doll house" of a home (264).
Two years older than Margaret, her only surviving sibling, Anna learns
quickly in life the necessity of putting things behind her, a lesson she
learns from her father (166). She considers herself unique, "not like
anyone else at all" (169), and her religious ecstasy increasingly takes
on a masochistic quality, as when her knees are gnarled from prayer
and her breasts and stomach covered with the "large suppurating
blotches" of the bites from red ants she forces herself to endure (307–
8). Indeed, her very aspect, as seen by her young son, is akin to the
mystically religious pictures one sometimes finds in the homes of the
very conventionally pious, and her eyes themselves start to "glitter,"
again the way such a painting would present a saint or a madonna.

All this is Anna's perverted way of supplicating God to allow
Anthony, dying of leukemia, to live, but her mothering is obviously
more a case of smothering. Her "dumb stoicism" (319) thus becomes
a form of mania, and after his disappearance and death she even contemplates his returning to fetus stage and then to sperm and egg. She
increasingly fantasizes about Anthony, seeing in her mind rows of candles and hearing bells (images of the Mass), seeing X-ray visions of
people around her, and even imagining "signs" of saints and others.
She is clearly obsessed, but the obsession results less, I believe, from the
death of Anthony than from the fact that now all of life is dead to her.
Robert is blatantly unfaithful, and she knows there will be no further
sexual or romantic relationship of any sort with him. When Robert
writes from the army to accuse her of letting Anthony die, she reflects,

We are all guilty, she thought; all the two-legged people tottering and strut-
ting on the crust of the earth. We never know what we do, never know what
sin. All of us. Even Anthony. The lovely lost boy. All the forked creatures,
stripped and naked. What did we do? The forked round skull, skin and hair
over it, camouflage. Circle of white bone, bottle of bone. Inside, the nameless
horrors. That no prayer or incense dispels. Thoughts like worms before the
grave.
    She was dead, she was dying, she was alive. The shapes faded, the bells
ceased, the flickering invisible candles turned back to air. (322)

And part of reality is Robert's coming back from the war to live with her, something she now looked forward to simply because she does not love him any longer and will have no further sexual contact with him, "like two animals trotting wearily in the same direction, untouching" (322). Love, for Anna, is now a burden she is happy to be rid of.

In the years that follow, Anna increasingly turns her attention toward constant remodeling and building of various residences and also to a foundation established by her father's wartime profits through which she is single-handedly effecting an economic revival in the local town. But her life is still untouched by reality; all her activity serves as a means of forgetting the horrors of her mind. As Margaret, her sister, observes, "Anna goes around building stage sets and then lives in them" (376), reminiscent of the joke that a neurotic builds castles in the air and that the psychotic not only builds these castles but also lives in them. Anna, though, maintains enough control so that she too can take an active role in her father's empire. And as her father is dying, Anna stands in such a way that Stanley can see not only the resemblance between her and Robert, but even more he can see her facial features which appear to the reader to be akin to the idealized religious pictures mentioned earlier, and with her "wide streak of gray hair [rising] sharply like a crest" (391), or, in other words, like a madonna's halo. Anna has always lived in the past and will certainly continue to do so in the years following her father's death, for she has absolutely nothing in life to look forward to, whether love or children or closeness to her sister or joy in having money. Her life is particularly pathetic, and Grau's success at creating such a believable character with so few strokes of writing is excellent.

C Margaret

As the younger of two children, Margaret early in life discovers that nothing in life was fair, particularly, in her case, because she feels that Anna had better physical features—beauty, shape, hair, eyes, and so forth (189). She also discovers that children are mean toward those less fortunate than themselves, and she thinks especially of a polio victim in her school who was perpetually taunted by the other girls. At Anna's wedding, Margaret, then still sixteen, drinks and tries in other ways to appear older than she is. She says then that she wants to be an old lady who tells dirty jokes to young boys (196), and she proves her daring by splashing around in a fountain with her party dress on. And then, as Anna embarks on her wedding-night with Robert, Margaret loses her virginity to her second-cousin's husband in the back seat of his car (197–98), obviously an adolescent method of "getting even" with her sister; even though she had expected a great deal from the act, she had in fact gotten nothing from it (201).

Margaret subsequently gets married several times, never for very long. Two days after high school graduation, she elopes, as her father had previously advised her to do; this marriage lasts only eight months. She then marries a New Yorker she meets in Paris, and they live in New York, where his father operates a restaurant, till he beats her up because of her promiscuity and she leaves him. In these and other relationships, she gradually realizes that she wants to be able to choose a lover as a man does, not to have to wait till she is chosen by a man (266–67); indeed, during her second marriage she had begun "collecting" lovers, by category. Always a "fool with men" (355), Margaret, when she finds herself pregnant, is completely unsure of the identity of the prospective father of her child.

Her relationship with brother-in-law Robert is particularly dramatic. When she first has sex with him, it is a mutual idea, even though she thinks of her first husband while they are together (251), but later Robert rapes her (361–62). Whatever romantic views she may have had regarding relations with males she loses following this rape, even though sex per se continues to be appealing on a nonpersonal level:

This is what age is, Margaret thought. . . . A slow diminution in feelings, in activities. . . . Her interest in men lessened. She admitted them to her bed more from habit than from raging desire. She still enjoyed the conjunction of bodies, but she no longer looked for any special value in their union. No longer did any shirt stretched over sweat-stained shoulders make her restless with desire. . . . But, curiously, her pleasure was greater than ever before. With precision, with experience, without passion, she arranged her orgasms into wide undulating bright-colored explosions. Proficiency and lack of real interest came together. She inspected each new male body carefully, detachedly, comparing it to others. No longer even seeing the individual. Her smooth appraising glance no longer saw a man, but a composite of all men, of male bodies. . . . (364)

Margaret's son Joshua, certainly knowing his mother's activities, grows increasingly apart from her, preferring to live with Anna and—not surprisingly—becoming more and more dedicated to a religious life based on the example of Dr. Albert Schweitzer. But when Joshua attempts to explain his faith to his mother, she is totally unreceptive and uncomprehending. Joshua at such times says to her, "You just don't understand" (357) and ". . . you make everything sound so cheap and horrible" (375), suggesting less that she fails to understand his idealistic impulses than that she has rejected idealism so totally in her own life.

For herself, there is the satisfaction of having money to spend, something considerably more appealing than the dead ideals of the past. In talking with her father, Margaret once observes that "money's like the yeast bread we learned to make in the convent, growing big and fat and swelling all out of the pans and bowls. Like it was alive, growing and creeping and walking. Like it was taking over the earth" (366). And this is in essence Margaret's use for money, a means toward lasting increases in the sheer quantity of pleasure available in life. She begins to collect art the way she had collected lovers, and she is completely happy in the process (367).

She subsequently shares with Anna the responsibility of managing the empire, and life goes on for her, if not completely fulfilled with another person, then at least free from despair and foolish entanglements. She is in most respects the son her father had wished for, and her commonsensical handling of the business becomes the continuation of the foundation he had laid. Margaret is infinitely more alive than her sister, though this vitality often takes the form of promiscuity and unwise relationships, and even in middle age, at the novel's end, she remains a far more substantial, earthy woman than her more ethereal sister.

D Robert

Robert Caillet, chosen by Oliver to be his "son" and successor, proves a far less wise choice than could have been foreseen. Just twenty-one when he first meets Oliver, Robert quickly proves that he can handle his work well and becomes Oliver's right-hand assistant. But the more he feels that "everything he'd ever wanted was within his reach" (156), the greater the degree of personal dissatisfaction he feels (216). Unlike the self-made Oliver, he seems incapable of escaping his origins. His Cajun heritage remains with him despite his successes, not merely as an alternate language he could swear in, but even more in that he simply will not allow himself to rise above the standards of his poverty-stricken background as a youth. In a conversation with Oliver, Robert acknowledges that he maintains a fondness for Cajun food such as gumbo and jambalaya. "You get so you like it," Robert says, "and then you keep on liking it all your life." After which Oliver says, pointedly, "*You* keep on liking it. That's your taste" (238–39), or, in other words, Robert insists on his relatively low-class taste even after he has moved into a world of affluence and taste.

Even worse, his moral taste remains common and crude even after he is selected to be Oliver's son-in-law. On his wedding-night, for instance, he makes love in his mind not with the lovely, innocent Anna lying next to him, but with the sluttish Betty, with whom he had had surreptitious, hurried sexual encounters standing in the dark outside her house. After "mounting" his wife (the choice of verbs is appropriately animalistic), he then slips to the floor to sleep, as he had been used to doing in his earlier, impoverished life. Angry with Anna when she discovers him on the floor, he thinks of what he had lost in his youth and shuts off all communication with her (226–27). His marriage to Anna, then, reminds him guiltily of where he had been and where he still truly belongs, so he spends the rest of his life attempting to recapture exactly the same level of crudity with which he had been raised. Three months after the wedding, Robert again makes love with Betty, and soon thereafter sets up a "fishing cabin" in the bayou to which he can take his "friends" for weekend trips, far away from Anna. In short, Robert is permanently and unchangeably in a moral— if not social—class far below the standards and values of any of the Oliver clan, including the "old man" himself, who had risen from much the same social class by his own struggles.

So insistent is Robert on demanding his own way, particularly in matters of sex, that several incidents occur in the book suggesting his basically subcivilized status. He perpetually connects innocence, in whatever form, with decadence such as his own; for example, after making love with Betty three months following the wedding, he then goes home to make love to his "doll wife" in their "doll house" (240). His demands on Anna's sister Margaret grow more and more insistent; the first time they have sexual intercourse, shortly after she is divorced and is at an emotional ebb, he is so frantic that he cannot even wait to take off his pants before mounting her (345). When she later berates him for being such a "lousy bargain" for her father to choose, he merely says, "Shut up and get on the sofa" (361), and he rapes her.

As his tastes run steadily more and more down toward total degradation, he observes:

Time was, two and three women a night didn't bother him. And a little something in the afternoon. God, he'd loved women, the shape of their asses under their skirts, the way their legs angled out. Most beautiful thing he'd ever seen. He remembered years ago, when he was still young enough to be taken to church, he'd seen written on the whitewashed walls in big black letters, CUNT IS GOD. (346)

Henceforward he wants younger and younger girls (fortunately for him, the state has a low age of consent), preferably virgins, and he first asks a madam to locate one for him (351–52) because, as he once cynically observes, "The little broads think I'm so cute; I'm the fatherly type. And it's funny how many of them want to screw their father . . ." (401). Small wonder, then, that he first recognizes the coming of middle age by the first gray pubic hair (394), and his insatiable erotic appetite grows, "down to a science" (245). As Anna spends more and more time in her various rebuilding projects, so Robert spends more and more time at his cabin or in dingy boardinghouses, "drowning in flesh" as a means of saying, "I am alive, I am here" (246). "Give me eight hours with a woman," he observes, "and I can have her. And it will be her idea, not mine . . ." (34).

Finally, though, Robert's lust simply diminishes, and "in the absence of lust there was only a great emptiness, a windy lightness, a giddiness" (340). He fills the emptiness with the fifty-five-foot cruiser subsequently named the *Condor*, and with the available, gullible young women who are impressed with his wealth and obvious status. So although the frequency with which lust drives his body is lessened, the intensity remains, and he continues to try one young woman after another, almost as if the *Condor* has given him a kind of youthfulness intended as a substitute for his dead son Anthony's eternal inability to love a woman.

Robert is particularly pathetic because he never discovers the true implications of love, not from his idealized mother raising him in poverty, not from his ascetic, perpetually virginal wife, not from his foster-father, Oliver, and certainly not from any of the myriads of bodies floating through his bed; Robert is most pitiable because he is incapable of feeling or of knowing love in any form other than physical.

When Oliver dies, Robert is effectively cut off from all decision-making responsibility regarding the family activities because of Oliver's agreement with his daughters. Far from a prude himself, Oliver was fully aware of Robert's uncontrollable lust and the driven way in which it took over all rational power from him; one speculates whether he will be able to remain the same thoughtless animal he has been with the transition of power to the two sisters, because their control will effectively reduce his financial independence and therefore his opportunities for casual sexual liaisons.

IV *The Condor as Symbol*

One point about *The Condor Passes* repeatedly criticized in reviews is Grau's rather heavy-handed use of the condor[4] as a symbol. Denis Donaghue, for example, commented, "I can't see that the symbol does anything for the book, and Miss Grau comes back to it at the end for no good reason.[5] Indeed, a good deal of the negative criticism accorded the book seems to have come because of this symbol, which simply does not work very well. In the novel, it is used first merely as a reference to Oliver's youthful travels to Chile and Peru, when he had seen the great birds soaring high above the mountains, a memory which so impresses him that he consciously uses the reference later as a name for his magnificent yacht. Robert subsequently has the name imprinted on everything identified with the boat—life preservers, china, glassware, sheets, towels (18)—thus making the name "condor" little more than a romantic motif, as a reference backward in time to Oliver's youthful wanderings.

Grau, though, was not content with using the condor merely as a motif of this sort; she also tried—unsuccessfully, I would say—to use it to refer to two quite dissimilar persons in the novel. In the first and more obvious case, it simply refers to the Old Man himself, sitting vulturelike, seemingly impassive and uncomprehending (as when Robert brings a young girl aboard the boat, intending to seduce her) but in reality taking in everything through his "bright black eyes." Similarly, the Old Man is described, shortly before his death, as having piercing black eyes, as being so frail and light that the wind could lift him aloft, and so on, thus clearly suggesting a parallel between him and a condor.

Even though this process of using the condor as a name seems to have come out of the Old Man's old-age reveries, Grau's application of the term to him, though somewhat strained, does seem possible. But her application of the term to another character is considerably less justified. Stanley, Oliver's black chauffeur and aide, who is so valued that he is willed land worth over a million dollars at the Old Man's death, is expected, in addition to his regular duties in which he is to be as unobtrusive as possible, to perform one particular task each day. The Old Man spends his waking hours, like similar characters in Raymond Chandler's *The Big Sleep* (1939) and elsewhere, in a warm, humid greenhouse in which a cageful of songbirds sings incessantly. Because of the cage's design, the birds have a high mortality rate, and so Stanley has to remove the dead birds, or kill and remove the obviously weakened ones, each day prior to Oliver's being wheeled into the greenhouse. As a "black birdman" (5), Stanley is like a "big hawk," "Grabbing up bits and pieces of things . . . the secret thief, that steals what people don't miss. . . ." (29). As such, Stanley is identified with both death and scavenging, characteristics also accorded the condor.

In the original short story subsequently expanded into *The Condor Passes*, there is also a reference to a black bird whose "black shadow . . . passed over the glass roof of the greenhouse"[6] as both a foreshadowing of the coming of death to the Old Man and a suggestion of Stanley himself. The Old Man talks about condors to Stanley in the story version, unlike the novel, and one of the first acts that Stanley performs in the story, immediately after the Old Man's death, is stealing one of his expensive cigars, a symbolic act of scavenging. In both versions, Stanley plans to leave the house permanently now that the Old Man is dead. In the novel, the last lines—floodlights casting Stanley's shadow on the path like a shadow of "black wings fluttering on each side" (421)—suggest that whatever role Stanley might have had as "condor" remains unchanged even after the Old Man's death, but there is nothing in the novel to suggest that such is the case.

And although Stanley, relatively uncomprehending, believes that it is he who is "the big black hawk spying on people's lives" (35), while at the same time rejecting such identification, it has in reality been the Old Man who best fits this description. Fully aware of the failings of others—their avarice, their hatred, their lust, their isolation, the Old Man reveals nothing of his motives until it is too late, as when he decides to cut Robert out of his will.

When the Old Man talks with Stanley about the condors, moreover, he mentions that gold dust was kept in the condors' feathers, to which Stanley responds with a shiver of the hairs on his neck: "He's looking at me, Stanley thought. Me, the big black bird. Where you going to put the gold, Mr. Oliver? Mr. Oliver, I ain't got no feathers to put gold dust in. I ain't your condor, so stop looking at me" (398). Stanley, missing much of Oliver's intent, infers that this is a reference to death (400) and that Oliver, senile, is trying to keep Stanley permanently in his control (403). So intent is Stanley in rejecting his inferred identification with condors that he himself becomes obsessed with it, thinking, just before Oliver's death: "Stanley looked at his own hands. They had come to rest on the rail of the bed, the black fingers were curved around the iron, gripping like claws. He saw himself a bird, a big black bird, perched on the Old Man's bed, waiting. . . ." (413). But waiting for what? The condor had been the Old Man's reverie alone, and was subsequently attached by the Old Man to his boat as a memento of his youth and as a suggestion that it, like the condor, carried "gold" (the Old Man himself?); at no time does the Old Man identify Stanley as the condor.

It is not that such application could not work, though Stanley does seem too insignificant a character for this to have major symbolic value. Rather, it is that the condor is used for too many dissimilar ends at once in the novel. As a symbol of death, it works quite well, with the Old Man's application of the term to his boat a suggestive reminder that all must die, his way of saying "Memento Mori." As a parallel in the same way to suggest the transport of wealth (gold dust in the condor's wings), it can also serve (but does not) as an effective suggestion of the transitory nature of wealth. But when it is arbitrarily applied to both the Old Man and to Stanley, then the condor simply becomes unconvincing and a needless burden on a novel otherwise relatively free of such symbolic touches; in a sense, the condor thus becomes an albatross.

V Evaluation

Much of the foregoing suggests that *The Condor Passes* was a significant falling-off from the forcefulness and richness of *The Keepers of the House*, and this is indeed the case. The later book has numerous failures both in conception and as finished novel, not the least of which are the use of the condor as symbol, the relatively one-dimensional characters (characters noted for their manifestation of a single overpowering impulse, such as masochism, avarice, lust, etc. rather than fully developed persons who come alive for the reader), and a very shadowy picture of the world of professional crime.

Even more, the book does not make as full use of the setting as one would have expected from Grau. There is no necessary reason why the novel is set in New Orleans and the Mississippi delta region of the gulf, nor is there any of the tie-in with or reference to the Sicilian gangs in New Orleans of the 1890s that brought the Mafia to American attention decades before present-day attention focused on crime; in the earlier case, nineteen Sicilian immigrants were arrested as conspirators in gang-warfare, with eleven of these killed by protesters who broke into the prison, leading, among other things, to Italy's cessation of diplomatic relations with the United States. If it was indeed true that "it was many years before law-abiding Sicilian and Italian immigrants felt at home in New Orleans,"[7] one cannot help but wonder why at least some of this factual material about Italians in the city was not reflected in the novel.

Furthermore, since most of the book is flashback to Oliver's youth, one tends to see him as either the dying nonagenarian or as a young man forced to rise by the established principles of the American dream, through hard work, taking advantage of the opportunities that come his way, thrift, prudence, and general perseverance. Though much of his fortune has been made through "illegal" means, such as liquor-running during Prohibition, this was true also of a number of more highly visible, respected Americans; thus, Oliver never seems like a "criminal," despite his being involved in several different illegal activities. It is difficult to think of him as a man who would forcibly remove those in his way or be guilty of any of the other machinations attributed to professional criminals, not only because Oliver is an insubstantial character, but even more because he is one thing for the reader and is said to be another by the author—a creative failure, on both counts. As Denis Donaghue astutely observes, "*The Condor Passes* is all foreground, very little background, everything is presented with the same degree of lucidity.... But after a while the lucidity begins to oppress...."[8]

Some aspects of the book are successful, but not the motivations determining the actions of the characters. Though Oliver and his daughter Margaret are potentially rich and alive, both serving as bundles of complex emotions surpassing easy description or summary, *why* they did what they did is never sufficiently discussed. Though Anna is perhaps as rich an assembly of potentially explosive forces as her father, she loses much of her maniacally driven desire to possess everything around her when this possessiveness leads to her son's death, and she is subsequently a lonely, masochistic woman.

But Grau's pacing of the novel, the way in which she controls her materials, judiciously rationing them out, character by character, is professionalism at its highest. The book is economical and spare, yet full enough in some important particulars to enable the reader to be aware of her major emphases, even though this very spareness may also, ironically, be the reason for the lack of depth perceptions into

Oliver's world or the motivations governing his rise to power. For the most part she lets the characters tell their own stories, a generally effective method of narration, but one that fails to work as well as it might when significant lapses occur in the characters' revelations to the reader. For there is no easy way in which these kinds of details can be provided other than through the characters' own reflections, unless one were to do as Grau did in *The Keepers of the House* and her subsequent novel, *Evidence of Love,* that is, to have various overlapping perspectives give us alternative interpretations of the characters' lives and actions.

The reader cannot but feel that a good many of the negative comments prompted by this novel were somewhat misdirected, since they all too often dwelt on what Grau did not do instead of what she did do. Her overall accomplishment, in retrospect, was slight when compared to her previous novel or to her first one, but it was a change of pace for her, one that perhaps did not work so well after the fact as it may have promised to do before.

The Condor Passes remains all in all one of her less significant works, for despite its brisk sales and book-club adoption, critics pointed out deficiencies in it that, again in retrospect, were always present to some extent in Grau's work—her inability to plot her novels as well as one would like, or her sometimes melodramatic handling of character interactions. While it remains not so bad as critics sometimes said and not so good as its *Book-of-the-Month Club News* promotion, it is nonetheless one of Grau's less notable novels, all the more so when it is compared with her subsequent *Evidence of Love.*

CHAPTER 6

Evidence of Love

G RAU once commented that she hoped one day to write a book that did not necessarily deal with the South,[1] presumably to indicate that her interests and themes were far more universal than a mere "regional" label might indicate. Certainly, the fact that most of her books are set in the South does not diminish their treatment of universal issues and emotions, yet when she attempts a novel not so located, she is still criticized for not sticking to what she presumably knows best. One critic noted that *The Condor Passes* was just one more "mess of gumbo"[2] and that Grau simply had little to say to the rest of the country, while another pointed out that she was on "unfamiliar ground"[3] in *Evidence of Love* by attempting a novel set in an area other than the Louisiana bayou country, forgetting, as Grau has noted on many occasions, that she has always lived in two locations and that for many years she has spent part of each year in the North, on Martha's Vineyard, as well as having spent shorter periods of time in various other locations. Of course, all of this proves nothing in and of itself regarding Grau's ability to locate a novel convincingly in the North, only that in her attempting to do so, some critics thought she was out of place.

But setting in Grau's 1977 novel, *Evidence of Love,* as in *The Condor Passes,* is of less importance than Grau's effectiveness in delineating the lives of people caught up in that setting. And a novel concerned with showing how certain specimens of humanity demonstrate their lack of any "evidence of love" for each other—whether the relationship be father-son, father-mother, husband-wife, or lover-lover—can as effectively be set in one locale as another. This, then, is Grau's only book set in the North (Philadelphia and elsewhere in the Pennsylvania–New Jersey area, in the approximate area where Rider College, which awarded Grau and her husband honorary degrees in 1973, is located), with brief passages in Chicago, London, and Africa as well. It is also the only book she has written to be published in a limited edition for collectors before the regular trade edition was published.

And, unlike the generally mixed-to-hostile reception accorded *The Condor Passes*, the critical acclaim given *Evidence of Love* was considerably more enthusiastic, with many critics considering the book among the best she had done.

I   *Plot and Structure*

Edward Milton Hanley, born on May 26, 1883, serves as the focal point in *Evidence of Love*, with first-person narratives by Henley opening and closing the novel and with similar first-person commentaries by Henley's son Stephen and Stephen's wife Lucy inserted. But it is Henley the father who dominates the successive generations of Henleys, much as Thomas Henry Oliver did in *The Condor Passes* and William Howland in *The Keepers of the House*. Grau's epigraph, from Wallace Stevens' poem "Le Monocle de Mon Oncle," fits Henley remarkably well as an indication of both his quest and his failure in making that quest:

> . . . I pursued,
> And still pursue, the origin and course
> Of love, but until now I never knew
> That fluttering things have so distinct a shade.

Both Stevens' poem and Grau's novel celebrate the mature man's contemplation of his youthful enthusiasms and joys. In common with other works celebrating the wisdom of maturity as contrasted with the lusts of youth—W. B. Yeats' *Sailing to Byzantium* is another work of this kind—Stevens seems to suggest that life's ultimate meaning resides in man's contemplative evaluation of his life from the perspective of maturity, with the diminishing of youthful lusts especially singled out as necessary for the development of inner perception and, therefore, wisdom.

Henley's birth, noted by his own father's inability, like that of Thomas Henry Oliver in *The Condor Passes*, to be present during the birth, is notable primarily because Henley describes, with total "recall," the circumstances surrounding the delivery. In a realistic novel, this may seem a bit farfetched, though in a work operating on a more surrealistic level, such as Tristram Shandy's recalling his own conception, this can be effective. Such a memory can also be expressed in a person obviously disturbed, as Grau demonstrated in the case of

Anna in *The Condor Passes,* who deliriously thinks back progressively to her dead son's childhood, infancy, development as a fetus, and finally individual sperm and egg. Nonetheless, Henley offers the description of the birth, presumably as a means of referring to an ugly porcelain bowl in which three generations of Henleys had been washed, and which he sentimentally puts in the same place in all the offices he has throughout his life.

The life shared by Henley's father and mother, no doubt rejected as a pattern of marital bliss by most contemporary couples, was one in which the father found his men's club more congenial than his home and in which his mother discreetly said nothing regarding the choice. Henley describes his parents as being like "aging animals," regarding each other as a "thoroughbred," as a "prized possession, an object whose value far exceeded its size," or as "a perfect diamond, to cherish and protect" (7).[4] The quality of the "love" shared by these two people, obviously, differs from that shared by the other characters in this novel but is evidently all too common in upper-class families of the era, and is used by the younger Henley as justification for his own inability to love:

She [the mother] no longer filled his [the father's] bed, but she filled his life. Perhaps that is not affection or love, but it is a recognition of value. And it is very durable, very durable indeed. Because it is based on a sense of propriety. Perhaps too that is why my marriages never succeeded. I was born completely without any sense of propriety. Any at all. (7)

Hence in the novel's first few pages we are given several telling characteristics of Edward Milton Henley based on his own parentage, which are to typify much of his subsequent life and especially his peculiar convictions regarding "love" toward those sharing his later life; he has no sense of propriety, he has little sense of duty, he is indifferent to others' values or desires, and he sees human relations in terms of their monetary worth. Indeed, the very christening service of the child, held after the hot summer months are passed, is notable more because Henley's father transferred half the family railroad interests to the child's name, which the narrator—ironically or not cannot be determined—says was "evidence of his love" (8), one of many echoes of the novel's title to be found in its pages.

As a child, Henley was raised by his mother to do the "Christian thing" in any situation in which he found himself, but, with a touch of

both childish rebellion and dedicated individuality, he says he has simply chosen not to do so (11). Even as a child and young man, Henley
is fully, consciously aware of his future, aside from those "miserable
two-legged annoyances" (i.e., other people) with whom he has on
occasion been forced to share both his bed and his life (14). It is for this
seemingly insensate reason that Henley feels and expresses no particular anguish at his sister's drowning on the *Titanic:* once she is gone,
she is beyond his interest. Again, as a touch of self-justification, he
observes, immediately after commenting on his sister's death, that his
family has always been "loosely connected" (16). Even when he is sick
almost to the point of death as a child—one of his recurring dreams is
of being dead—it serves less as an occasion to draw him, the sole
remaining child, closer to his parents than it is to draw him to their
disinterested attention. Sent to a sanitorium in Switzerland, Henley sees
those around him as "barbarous" and the women he has his first sexual
adventures with as merely aphrodisiac in nature, not as human beings.
At age nineteen he is sent to study in Leipzig, and though he shares
the carousing of his university fellows, he resists any sort of permanent
attachment, something he says he has never liked (29). Hence his parents' death, requiring his taking over the family enterprises, becomes
as ephemeral and shallow a commitment as any he has had previously,
though he does run the businesses profitably. He meets his first wife,
Abigail, in Chicago and marries her in California, discovering in his
desire to father a child a degree of conventionality that he had neither
known of nor suspected (39). But his method of assuring himself of an
heir is far from conventional: he finds the "perfect incubator" for a
child, a young Irish girl "of no importance whatever," an intelligent
sixteen-year-old virgin who is paid ten thousand dollars for the "business deal" by which Edward has a son (40); the son, Stephen, becomes
the second narrator of the book. Edward and Abigail divorce, and he
marries Eleanor Halsey, with whom he spends the longest time with
any of his wives, evidently a few years.

Stephen, in his turn, becomes many of the things his father could
not accept, leading the older Henley to contemplate a "defeat" by
genetics (43). Stephen is the completely rational, dedicated scholar in
prep school and at Princeton University; for him "the pursuit of knowledge is [his] love" (45), and he subsequently becomes a Unitarian minister, a church the elder Henley does not consider "respectable." Stephen's total personal privacy takes the form of not even telling his
father of his own marriage, to Lucy Roundtree Evans, till two days

before the event. When they meet, Henley dislikes her at once and even attempts to offend her by asking whether she is pregnant. But Stephen and his wife, completely the aloof, sensible couple, merely answer the impertinent question coolly and dispassionately, indicating by this, and by the refusal of any financial assistance from the elder Henley, that they wish to be as independent as possible from him.

When the marriage between Edward Milton Henley and Eleanor ends, Henley chooses Guido O'Connor as his lover, one, he says, of only three or four men he has had as lovers in his entire life. Then he marries Lenore, a German, for six months, and Sara, for an equally short period. And then he meets but does not marry Helen Reed because, as he says, with the coming of age one becomes more wary (52). The "most breathless woman" he had ever known, Helen's sheer intellectual excitement exhausts Henley into indifference (52), and this match too ends. For, as Henley reflects,[4] "When I love, I don't want to think that very soon I shall be hating. I want to think that each love is eternal, that we shall live happily together ever after. Even when I know perfectly well that we shall not" (54). Hence in his old age Henley chooses Roberta as his mistress; together for six years, she is barely thirty, a "veritable infant" to the old man (55). But this too, he knows, will end; following his recovery from a heart attack, he decides to rid himself of her, knowing he will miss her merely because she was so "decorative" (57). But he will not miss her nearly as much as he once might have, because he has grown weary of women, preferring, now that he is quite aged, the company of his four great-grandchildren. And at this point Stephen's narrative takes over.

Stephen's narrative begins when he is sixty years old, enduring asthma, emphysema, and diabetes, among other ills. And he is getting forgetful, but not so forgetful that he cannot relate his own recollection of growing up a Henley. He knows, for example, that as he ages he will become an object of pity, unlike his father, who would inspire only anger and hatred in others. Indeed, Stephen seems considerably more aged and even senile than his vigorous father. Stephen does see that his father's great strength comes from being able to see things in life singly and to act on them accordingly (62), whereas the younger Henley has to embellish everything. And the day he begins to narrate his version of the family story is the day he is asked by the police to come to try to talk three holdup men from a school where two classes of young children and two nun teachers are being held hostage. A celebrity and unwilling hero following the ordeal in which one holdup man is killed and the other two captured, Stephen returns home in time to receive a call from his father congratulating him on his "impressive," "courageous," and "heroic" performance.

But Stephen sees no cause to be proud of what he has done—in the ordeal or in life. He knows his father has been a collector of beautiful women, and though he admires beauty, he is not "moved to possess them in any way" because sex is a "waste of energy, too time-consuming and too complicated" (75). As a prep-school youth, he had had one intense, desire-filled relationship with a woman, and though satisfying, the desire was gone once the act of sex had been realized; it was as if he had been "born and died at once" (83). Even in his marriage, it is a relief when they grow tired of each other's bodies. And when Stephen realizes that it is the end of desire, he then feels "an echoing surge, a shadow of a dimly remembered burst of joy and power, . . . a ghost of a shadow of the beginning" (83). Even in this, he realizes, he is looking for the end, and he knows he has reached it with a "far faint echo of happiness" (83).

When Stephen decided to marry Lucy, he was already twenty-six years of age and minister of the Unitarian Church in Shelby, Pennsylvania; Lucy had been teaching at Greenwood College in Virginia. He immediately felt a sense of "familiarity" with her; without "undue passion," the two marry on June 21, 1939, they have two sons, Thomas and Paul, both grown, and now, toward his own life's end, he can summarize thirty-four years of marriage with one sentence: "We met, we married decently, we bred, and we are now about the business of growing old and dying" (87). Retired and living in Florida, Stephen and Lucy are ending their days in the "elephant graveyard" together, with Stephen completing various classical studies begun earlier. The sons follow their own impulses; Thomas, Stephen's favorite, rejects his father's emphasis on rationality and assumes some of his own grandfather's promiscuity, while Paul, more the emotional sort, grows up to live in a Chicago high-rise apartment house and collect the work of an obscure primitive painter.

Following his retirement from the ministry, acknowledged by a gala ceremony with the elder Henley present along with many dignitaries, Stephen and Lucy move to Florida, where Stephen continues to translate from the classics with the assistance of a priest from a local Roman Catholic college where Stephen himself begins to teach Greek. In visiting Paul and his family in Chicago, Stephen and Lucy are constrained to look at some sixteen paintings by an obscure painter, one of whose paintings has persuaded Paul that the artist was Stephen's own mother, Edward's "incubator" for a child when he was married to Abigail (41). But Stephen does not react as Paul had hoped, for he does not demonstrate any particular interest in the woman he now finds, when he is already an old man, was the mother he had never known. Paul, shattered at the rejection (of himself and his quest as much as of the nameless woman), says nothing, but Stephen knows the extent to which his son has been injured by the rejection.

Nonetheless, life goes on in Florida for Stephen and Lucy, and as they age they occasionally acknowledge candidly the disappointments they had experienced in life, such as Lucy's belated announcement that she had secretly hoped, years before, for six children. One day, when Lucy is at a meeting, Stephen goes as usual to his desk, feeling vaguely uncomfortable; sensing only quiet and darkness, unable to see even the neighbors' lights or to hear their automobile's engine, he tries to open the door but cannot; he tries to remember his wife's name but cannot; he turns the flashlight full on his face but sees nothing in the glass reflecting his image; and he gasps, knows what he had come there to do (137). Like his namesake, the first Christian martyr, Stephen dies, as he lived, in pursuit of the truth.

"Stephen, how could you. I wasn't even home" are among Lucy's first words upon finding her husband's body. Her son Thomas reacts with bitterness and son Paul with "cosmic fear" at their father's death (142), and Stephen's father, too frail to travel, sends a film-crew to record the burial. And as the old man had agreed, Lucy will henceforth be cared for as a result of a trust fund he had established if she were to survive Stephen. But upon being told of the fund, the two sons break into argument, and when Thomas says that his mother will henceforth be rich enough to buy a new husband (148), Paul begins to fight with his brother. Afterward, contemplating her husband's death and the inevitable end for all life, Lucy thinks of her death as well.

And she reflects on her earlier life, especially about her first husband, Harold Evans, a brilliant archeologist who killed himself after he and Lucy had been married for only a short time. Early in their relationship Harold had come to Kenya, where Lucy had been living with her family, and there they had gotten married. His complete dedication to his research isolated Lucy, and thus she too began to study. The only time Harold came alive was in the dark, when they made love. But

Lucy "did not want to need anybody that much" and she began to find sex repellent (172); yet she finds herself desiring Harold at odd times, such as when she is driving; realizing that "no one man was so different from another" (175), she contemplates getting a lover but does not. When Harold goes to Sardinia, Lucy begins to write children's books, continuing to do so when Harold returns. Then, after an uneasy time together in which Harold is obsessed with the strain under which he has been living, as well as clearly disturbed by all that is identified with their home, he disappears and is found in the university auditorium, dead from a shotgun blast. Following the funeral, she sees his final manuscript through the publishing process and leaves, eventually teaching at Greenwood College in Virginia, where she meets Stephen Henley, with whom she spends the next thirty-four years as a minister's wife. Now, content and herself close to the end of her life, Lucy is perpetually called by her anxious sons. But, she says, "God save me from love. And the proof of love" (204), and, as she reflects again to the terrible urgency of physical love with Harold, she thinks again of the "evidence of love" (205), evidence that now seems so strangely part of the long-ago.

The final pages of the novel are again narrated by Edward Milton Henley, now over ninety years of age, bored with the travails of old age and the imminence of death: "How busy my death is. And how slow" (212). Thinking over his own past years, he realizes that he has never had a black man as a lover, though he had had black women, as well as many other shades (214). Paul confronts his grandfather with the picture he believes to have been painted by his own grandmother, but the old man says he does not remember what Stephen's mother looked like. Thomas comes to relate that his wife has left him to go to Caracas with a man she had had as a lover for over a year. But realizing that everyone's attention is designed as a way of preparing for his own death, the old man thinks sardonically about old loves, the equipment keeping him alive in his room, and such matters. Then Lucy comes to visit him and asks if he wants the Seconals lying near him that he has indeed desperately wanted as a way out of the prison of his own body. As he slowly sinks into oblivion, he sees Lucy sitting, reading a magazine and tries to call to her, but she is unable to hear him. He is dead, but for a few seconds again thinks back to a "perfect union" he had shared once in Mexico, many years earlier, through the medium of a pipe filled with opium or some such substance, claimed then and believed now to be "the gate of heaven" (227).

II   *The Characters*

As with *The Condor Passes*, this novel is dominated by the physical presence of one man who grows to epic proportions, although of less than ideal stature; he is, quite simply, the one indomitable individual in his world, and so it is no wonder that his more intellectual son chooses not to be like his father, not to accept aid from his father, and not even to allow his father entry into his more spiritual world. For Edward Milton Henley reminds us of another man with the same surname, William Ernest Henley (1849–1903), author of the inspirational poem "Invictus," and like the narrator of that poem, this novel's Henley is "the master of [his] fate" and "the captain of [his] soul." It is also not completely accidental that his middle name is Milton, for Henley, like Satan in Milton's epic, also rebels against whatever deity there is in order to choose his own way of life.

Henley has all that he wishes of the world's wealth, and although it is facile to say that he has "gained the world and lost his soul," the truth is that he has gained the world and *kept* his soul. That is, he is not controlled or manipulated by anyone or anything; he makes his own life and governs it by his own machinations; he loves whom and when and how he pleases, regardless of conventional morality; and he dies unrepentent and longing still for the glorious days when he was young and vigorous. He, of course, feels that his money can buy him anything he wants, and to some extent he is correct; but he cannot buy the love of his son or of any of the women—or men—he has had as lovers. In short, he is the complete loner, and though one can project and say that his solitude is its own punishment, he does not seem to be too unhappy with the way his life has turned out. His pleading for Seconal at the novel's end is itself not a sign of dependence or weakness or escape so much as it is an acknowledgment that he has no more life, only a vegetable existence, and that Seconal is the only way out. Ironically, his grandsons are so caught up in their own problems and frustrations that they do not see their grandfather's deathbed need; all they can do is to comment on their own problems. It takes the plain, unassuming, intelligent Lucy to see that her father-in-law longs for the same end that her own husband has gone to.

Stephen, in fact, is somewhat like his namesake, the first martyr of the early Christian church, even though his particular brand of religion, Unitarianism, is more humanistic than Christian. Still, he is a dedicated man, aware of his frailties, even more aware of the extent to which he could be overshadowed by his father if he would only relent enough to let his father have any sort of influence in his life, and most of all aware of the fact that his path in life, that of a scholar, is far from the gregarious *joie de vivre* his father emanates in his financial successes and personal encounters. More than once in the novel Stephen realizes that he is old before his time; with his plan for life (92), he had organized everything to such a degree that, among other things, he realized if he did not marry by a certain age he would never marry. This highly disciplined, organized approach to life is obviously far from the spontaneous, seemingly chaotic life experienced by his father. Hence the contrast between the elder Henley's promiscuous love-life and Stephen's own calculated, rational decision for a wife is all the more striking.

At twenty Stephen had been more intelligent and perceptive than at any other time in his life, and he then regularly jotted down his "ideals" in the endless journals, which he of course shows to Lucy before their marriage so that she has a complete idea of who and what he is. But the ideals he has tried to live by do not get passed on to their sons, for Thomas becomes more like the oldest Henley and Paul more like someone afraid of acknowledging either kind of forebear. On a pop-psychology level one could say that Edward Milton Henley and grandson Thomas reflect more of the id than anything else, and Stephen more of the superego; but then one wonders where to put grandson Paul, since he seems wholly afraid of seeming rootless or without a direct line of descent into the past. Hence Paul, by far the most overtly troubled male member of the three generations, seems more intent on forcing the past into the lives of those in the present who really do not share his obsession. Thomas, by contrast, is much more directionless and floundering than anyone else in the family: when Stephen shows Thomas the journals, Thomas' reaction is to ask "Why set up laws to tyrannize yourself?" (93), to which Stephen, naturally, replies by pointing out that rationality was not the same as tyranny. Then Stephen makes the pointed remark, one that says much about both of them: "Thomas, you need not agree with my principles. But why do you feel called upon to change my way of thinking in order to justify yours?" (93). The answer is that although rationality works as a method of adapting to life for Stephen, it is completely unworkable as a system for the more emotional Thomas. And whereas the oldest Henley is completely and happily hedonistic, Thomas is the genetic throwback who, skipping his father's generation, now attempts unsuccessfully to resemble his grandfather. But Thomas is not and cannot be as completely a seeker after pleasure as his grandfather, as we see especially clearly when Thomas' wife leaves him and he reacts with such bitterness that he even brings his own sons into the fray, forcing them through appropriately worded questions to choose sides between himself and his departed wife.

Another way of distinguishing among these hapless persons is by contrasting them on the basis of one statement about Edward Milton Henley: Stephen's comment that his father "did not feel guilt or remorse. His deepest emotion was amusement—he had in a sense lived a life with one theme, comedy" (77). Indeed, the elder Henley seems to treat all those within his range with the same kind of amused contempt, a condescending expression of their innate inferiority compared to his own vigorous self-reliance. But Stephen seems completely humorless, never seeing the absurdity of the human condition, never adopting a wry manner as an antidote to the chaos and confusion of his life. Even when he serves as go-between with the holdup men and the police, he acts completely the rational man-of-the-cloth who has had a long and full life and who therefore is not hesitant to die if necessary in doing his duty. At least the holdup men are willing to die for the style of life they have chosen, unlawful as it may be; but Stephen lives for no emotional impulse, merely for the sense of having followed the guidelines laid down so carefully and rationally in his journals or in the three decades and more of sermon preparation. Even the ceremony acknowledging the end of his long service to his church seems to leave him unmoved—at least by comparison to the way in which a more normally balanced person would have reacted. Though Stephen does not believe in sin (76), he does believe in propriety—hence his implicit judgment through his life toward his father and his father's conventionally immoral existence.

Similarly, Stephen's two sons seem incapable of recognizing the essential absurdity, and therefore comedy, of life. For Paul, things hurt too much for him to laugh, and so he cries, cries especially when it comes to trying to dredge up a past that had lain dead for half a century and which should have remained dead even then. Thomas, who tries to be as promiscuous, at least in intent, as his grandfather, sees nothing whatever ironic in his wife's leaving him for a secret lover with whom she has maintained an affair for a year; nor does he react with anything resembling justifiable anger or a changed perspective regarding people's infidelities. Instead, he feels sorry for himself, and through self-pity tries to expiate the sense of being wronged that her desertion has caused. In neither case do these grandsons maintain the sardonic, slightly amused, slightly contemptuous perspective of their grand-father.

Indeed, in the entire novel only one character comes close to being a figure of the same stature as Edward, and that is his daughter-in-law Lucy, who can see the irony of the life she spends with Stephen, who can comment jocularly years after the fact about suppressed desires that simply never became an issue of contention between herself and her husband, and who sees, alone of all those in the family, exactly what the effect of impending death is on a human being. For, after all, she is the only one who survived two mates, and though her two hus-bands differ sharply from each other—Harold the impetuous, impul-sive wanderer, Stephen the clear-headed, rational controller of his own life and desires—she never ceases thinking about both. The difference between her and the others in the book is that though she has the per-spective whereby she could maintain the same aloof attitude toward life and death as her father-in-law, she also has enough of the self-dis-cipline needed to manage her life the way she wishes, a way enabling her to combine the dead but appealing past with the alive but dull present. She could easily have gone the route of cynicism following Harold's suicide, but instead she threw herself into her work, first by seeing Harold's manuscript through to publication, then by continuing to write children's books, and then by recommitting herself to another man for a quite different kind of marriage.

Hence Lucy's question to her father-in-law regarding the Seconals is completely fitting and appropriate, for she alone can understand the mind of her father-in-law, can see that he loves life but has accepted the fact that life for him is over. Though her act of giving him the Seconals could be labeled a form of "mercy-killing," it is really much more than that (and far less than serving as an accomplice before-the-fact in aiding a person to kill himself); she knows the effect of suicide in a conventional sense, as when Harold killed himself by a shotgun blast. But Henley has lived a long and for him a full life, and is now ready to end on the same no-regrets level as he has lived. One cannot help but see that Lucy is doing the same thing she would hope someone would do for her if and when she is in the same situation, that is, to perform an act of mercy and kindness, even though it may not be deserved, to enable a person to die the way he wishes to die. And once Lucy makes the decision to help Henley, she goes on to whatever is next in her mind, seemingly unaware of his slipping into oblivion and seemingly unconcerned with the fact of death, unlike the more conventional nurse and housekeeper, who cry because it is expected of them.

In brief, Lucy is fully as honest as her father-in-law, though she has chosen a different method of maintaining her essential honesty, one requiring the openness of the elder Henley with the discipline and planning characterizing Stephen. And unlike her two sons, Lucy is completely free of the weak self-pitying of Thomas and the seeking after a possibly nonexistent past of Paul. She, like so many others of Grau's women characters, is a strong, relatively silent, and completely believable woman combining the virtues required for survival in a cynical, malevolent world quite different from the optimistic creed preached by her husband. In this she resembles Abigail Mason Howland, the narrator-protagonist of Grau's *The Keepers of the House*, and like her she goes about quietly changing those things she can. She is considerably stronger than her introverted husband Stephen, and only her father-in-law approaches her in personal vigor or resolve. Just as he is immediately impressed with her character when they first meet (86), so she knows him in an intuitive manner, too, knows the kind of man he is and the demons forcing him continually to try to find new and more extravagant forms of pleasure to make life bearable; the old man knows that she may marry again (203), and she knows that he is ready to die. Hence they are balanced in a way in which neither can dominate the other, though each knows the other's strengths and presumably the other's weaknesses as well.

Oddly enough, this novel was criticized by some reviewers for the "bloodless" characters it contains. True, the novel does strip away much of the sentimentally idealistic and even romantic paraphernalia of conventional life, but this is far from saying that these characters— Edward Milton Henley and his daughter-in-law Lucy at least—do not possess full-bodied, full-blooded personalities and existences. For it is closer to the truth to say that Grau examines and finds wanting some of the conventional role-playing between individuals, and that in so doing she uses certain situations between individuals as a means of showing how detached people can try to be when they are either too self-disciplined (like Stephen) or too resistant to the truth about the present (like either of the grandsons).

Only those who have lived a great deal, such as the elder Henley and Lucy, can resist a great deal of personal revelation by which their essential security in the world is destroyed or otherwise damaged. And though one may say that Lucy seems better able to adapt to the realities of the life she has chosen, on a realistic level, one cannot deny that the elder Henley has lived a full, vigorous, unrepentent life of pleasure, seeking after wealth and cynical detachment from most conventional values. Lucy's choice is doubtless the wiser choice for the majority of humans, but Henley's choice is the one that appeals the greater—*if* one were to carry it out without concern for convenional morality, religion, law, or retribution outside the control of great wealth. Since that is a very great "if," and since few persons can live lives of such luxurious indifference to conventional value-systems, Lucy's choice seems in most respects the better and more fulfilling one. While the other characters in this novel have their more direct parallels in one or another of Grau's novels, with Henley immediately reminding us of "the Old Man" in *The Condor Passes,* Lucy remains one of Grau's most striking and unique characters.

III   *Evaluation*

Grau's detailed portrait of members of a family in their various combinations of love and hatred becomes considerably more than a series of random observations regarding the decline and fall of a wealthy, jaded clan. The ironic title, in a sense, says it all: nowhere is there any "evidence of love" in the combinations of persons presented in the novel. Individually, certain types of love are possible, as in Lucy's basically dedicated nature or, in a different sense, in the elder Henley's hedonism. But love, to mean anything, must be seen in context with others upon whom the love is acted out or received; even hedonism becomes little more than a particularly obsessive form of masturbation if the practitioner seeks only and always to find merely his own satisfaction.

What Grau has given us is a particularly honest portrait of a family, each member of which (except for Lucy) is intent on seeking his own form of satisfaction to the exclusion of others. Even if this is justified in terms of a rational program for one's life, as with Stephen, it still becomes a form of self-aggrandizement and narcissism. It may well be that only the wealthy and religious in our society (to choose the categories in which Henley senior and Stephen fall) may elect to be so completely monomaniacal as to indicate their being led by forces larger than themselves; but in effect those in such categories become fully as self-centered as those with less "pure" motives. Grau strips these various forms of love from all their idealistic trappings and surroundings so that no remnants of genuine emotional commitment remain, and in this even Lucy seems less than ideal because of the compromises she had made to assure a continually happy marriage with Stephen. That is, all the narrators, including Lucy, remain so detached from their own lives that they cannot see—until it is too late for any effective alteration of tactics—what they are doing to themselves as well as to others. Each of the three voices in the narration is effective in terms of his or her own concerns, even though, as some critics noted, there is not a sufficiently distinctive style utilized for the three to make them clearly and distinctly unique from each other. If they are indeed "bloodless," then this is because they are so intent upon revealing their frustrated forms of "love" that whatever substance they may have had as characters is diminished.

In particular, ironies abound in Grau's somewhat clinical evaluation of the lack of any "evidence of love." Already mentioned have been such touches as the ironic use of proper names for some of the characters; even more of these, however, are to be found in the novel. For example, when Stephen and Lucy move to Florida in their retirement years, Stephen joins with a local priest to study Latin. Stephen, as suggested, is far more intellectually inclined than he is physically; physical love becomes for him one of the things he does not miss as he grows older. The priest, too, is presumably more dedicated to a life of Christian love than to its erotic counterpart. Hence when we read the priest's name (111) as David Harold Lawrence—another D. H. Lawrence— we are at the very least a bit taken aback because of the irony, conscious or unconscious, between what he stands for and what his literary counterpart, who called himself a "priest of love,"[5] often emphasized in his fiction. While one may pursue this too far, at the very least these names are suggestive and possibly even evocative of the traits of the characters to which they are attached.

Critics who emphasized Grau's change of setting, moreover, missed the substance of her emphasis in another way, because in changing the locale from the one more "typical" for a Southern writer, she in essence is showing the universality of the insights regarding human behavior and relationships that are at the heart of the novel. If, therefore, such observations as she makes are true in one locale, they are likely to be as valid in another as well. But the handling of the theme of love is considerably more mature and sophisticated than anything she had tried previously. The epigraph from Wallace Stevens again comes to mind: each of the characters in this book, including Lucy, continues to pursue "the origin and course / Of love," but without realizing that such insubstantial things as love in its different guises do indeed have an indistinct shadow or image. Love, therefore, can only be evidenced in such mutual encounters as enable both partners to grow effectively in the relationship, and this is simply not to be found in most of the combinations present in this book. Even Stephen and Lucy compromise their essential characters to some extent in choosing each other as mates, for neither can be totally honest until late in life, when passion is decayed and their lives almost over.

Furthermore, Grau presents most of the commonly accepted forms of love in the pages of this novel. The erotic is of course found primarily in the person of Edward Milton Henley, who seems willing to try any experience that occurs to him, but it is also present—or rejected—in the lives of all the others in the book. Some find that erotic love becomes a curse that follows them throughout their lives, as when Thomas' wife Claudia leaves him for another, presumably more desirable, man with whom she has maintained a clandestine sexual relationship for a year. Yet even rejecting the erotic as a form of love, as Stephen does to some extent, is tantamount to an acknowledgment that it is a form of love to which he cannot aspire.

On the other hand, the spiritual kind of love, with which Stephen seems reasonably well familiar, is wholly incomprehensible to his father. Paul knows primarily the love of seeking for roots in the past, but he too seems somewhat incapable of evaluating the necessary relationships in the present, as when he simply does not comprehend the kind of attention his mother needs following his father's death. Lucy also lives in the past, with her first husband Harold and the orgasmic pleasure thinking of him years later provides as contrasted with the more mundane, even dull, existence she shares with Stephen; yet she also knows the implications of a love greater than the physical, the kind of love that enables her to love and live with Stephen, to bounce back quickly after his death, and to give of herself when her father-in-law requires it. In fact, her actions in giving him the Seconals may well be the most vivid form of *agape* to be found in the book, in that her act is wholly selfless and lacking in personal gain of any sort. Stephen, by contrast, does offer himself to the police as an intermediary when he is needed to stop the holdup men from injuring or killing the school

children; yet, as his name implies, there is something of the martyr in
him in that he knows his long life is almost over and that he therefore
has nothing to lose were the holdup men to kill him. Selfless love of the
agape variety is probably the hardest kind to create believably in fiction, and Lucy seems, alone of all those in the book, to know what this
is and how to go about expressing it in a form of action.

While the tangled web of relationships in this novel is perhaps not
so intricately woven as in *The Keepers of the House,* which remains
Grau's finest novel to date, the emotional interrelationships in *Evidence of Love* come closer than anything else she has written to an
attempt to analyze character with the same degree of complexity as in
the earlier novel. These characters range the gamut of excesses of kinds
of love, yet none of them knows the meaning of love in the relationships that comprise the bulk of the book; even Lucy's most profound
awareness of love comes not from her relationship with Stephen but
with Harold, her suicidal first husband. This is not to say that the book
is a flawless performance, for, again as some critics noted, the three
voices are not sufficiently demarcated, there is too little positive substance to outweigh or even to balance the overwhelmingly negative
picture of human relationships, and the lush style, among Grau's most
evocative works in terms of sheer control of language, sometimes hides
the lack of depth in commitments made by the various characters. One
is never quite sure, for example, why Lucy marries Stephen, nor why
Paul attempts to recapture the past so obsessively as he does, nor why
Edward Milton Henley, patriarch of them all, becomes such a cynical
observer of humanity from afar; after all, there is nothing unusually
decadent in his conventional parents' lives to suggest that he suffered
some particularly traumatic moment that causes him to seek only physical satisfaction and to distrust all other forms of love. Yet these are
presented as axiomatic in the novel, they are presented as "givens" we
must accept, and they thus become the kinds of details about character
that ultimately resist analysis.

Another point of comparison with *The Condor Passes* is the fact
that both novels are greatly expanded versions of previously published
short stories. As the previous chapter indicated, a story named "The
Condor Passes," renamed "Stanley" when published in book form as
part of a collection of stories, became the nucleus for the basic plot and
part of one major section of *The Condor Passes*. In much the same
way, an earlier story entitled "The Patriarch"[6] served as the nucleus

for *Evidence of Love*. The original story begins, as does the novel, with
Edward Milton Henley providing a dramatic monologue in which he
tells of his early life, his various loves and wives, the birth of his only
son, and the son's eventually becoming a Unitarian minister; the story
ends with the son's reflecting on his father's hedonistic values and his
own sons' playing in the garden with their grandfather, with the elder
Henley's wave interpreted by the minister as "altogether like a
blessing."

As a story, "The Patriarch" is not particularly distinguished, at least
in part because the focus shifts from the pleasure-seeking elder Henley's perspective (for whose confessional reverie we have no valid
explanation anyhow), and in part because the son and his family seem
an unnecessary intrusion upon the old man's reflections. One major
change does occur in the transformation from story to novel, however,
and that is in the son's name being changed from Anthony in the short
story to Stephen in the novel. (Grau also changes the ungrammatical
"The Reverend Henley" in the story to the more precise "The Reverend Mr. Henley.") Nonetheless, the story does suggest that Grau's original conception of the elder Henley was not materially altered in the
expansion from story to novel.

The form of *Evidence of Love*, finally, is clearly the same as that
used by Grau in *The Keepers of the House* and *The Condor Passes*:
several distinct personalities speak successively to offer overlapping,
contrasting interior monologues on the central events and relationships
in their respective loves. While this was not so effective as it could have
been in *The Condor Passes*, it is considerably more successful in *Evidence of Love*, covering, as it does, a number of disparate personalities
involved over many years with many other persons and places. For the
reader comes to know these several narrators as well as he is to know
any fictional figures in Grau's collected work, and the feeling the
reader inevitably has at the novel's conclusion is akin to having old
acquaintances gradually fade away and die. While Grau's achievement
is hardly unflawed (for example, all three narrators sound, to some
extent, like each other, with the same vocabulary and intonations), for
the most part the novel succeeds quite well in demonstrating that her
mastery of form, pacing of narrative, and manipulation of character
were as under control as in her first books.

Following the publication of *The Condor Passes*, it was mentioned
on occasion that Grau had no more to say, that her concern with her

own part of the country and the tangled webs of racial and other forms of distrust among people were all she had to write about. If anything were needed to suggest that Grau had more substance as a novelist than these statements, it was *Evidence of Love*. It may well be that as a novelist she may either cease to develop or may take an entirely different direction from that indicated by anything she has published to date. After a book such as this, however, it is certainly entirely too early to write her off as a "one-novel" author who ends up saying the same thing again and again.

CHAPTER 7

Short Stories

OF THE many short stories written by Grau since she began writing professionally (that is, omitting those done for university or amateur publications in New Orleans), nine were collected in her first book, *The Black Prince and Other Stories*, and eighteen in her second collection, *The Wind Shifting West*. Since the stories in these two collections are among the most representative stories Grau has written, the comments in this chapter will indicate the range and merit of her shorter fiction.

When asked about her short stories, Grau replied that she thought "the short story as a form is lacking," and that

It's easier to do a story, because you can in a sense get your hands around it, you can get hold of it, the bones are more visible, it makes a more pleasing shape. You tend to see the skin, the structure, the shape of short stories more easily, and this is more pleasing to the aesthetic sensibility. In a novel, unless it's a very short one, you just don't see the structure, and so it's not as aesthetically pleasing. But it's a matter, I think, of what you value. The novel, because it's longer, can generate a lot more power, and in my old age I'm beginning to be more and more conscious of that power, of power and intellectual content. I think, for example, that Eudora Welty has beautiful structure, but she completely lacks drive or power; she doesn't generate anything. And as much as I dislike Faulkner, at times he does generate quite a sense of a force moving, and I don't think you ever get that in a short story.[1]

While Grau once published four or five stories a year (in 1961 and 1962), more recently she has scarcely published any, in part, no doubt, because many of the traditional markets for short stories are disappearing or drying up, with the demise of magazines like the old *Saturday Evening Post*. Also some of the markets that formerly were more concerned with good fiction than with any specific audience, like the traditional "women's magazines," have increasingly narrowed their perspectives and chosen fiction geared to particular groups of readers.

I The Black Prince and Other Stories

Grau's critically acclaimed first book seems in retrospect the kind of talented though contrived collection of lyrical tales so often identified with a youthful writer. Her sharp awareness of sensory stimuli, particularly the visual, is evident in most of the stories in the book, as is her fairly obvious use of symbolism, particularly symbolism based on biblical or other traditional sources. The frequent lack of any substantial plot in these stories, or of plots lacking any legitimately developed conclusions, may attest to their author's relative inexperience as a writer of fiction, but even so the tales are finely etched, intuitive glimpses of life in the rural South, often with impoverished blacks as characters, and with Grau's consistently fine sense of atmospheric detail always present. Certain touches seem contrived; for example, almost every story features some object or other that is a glittering silver color.

In general, the stories in this collection that are concerned with blacks are more effective than those concerned with whites; the former seem imbued with a sense of mystery, with echoes of folklore and myth often emphasized. She handles dialect well, and she never sentimentalizes or patronizes her characters. She creates believable, well-rounded human beings, people who, regardless of color or social level, remain firmly memorable. In short, with her first book Grau made a solid though not flashy or spectacular debut as a writer. Although only three of the stories had appeared separately in periodical form before the appearance of the collection in book form, most of the nine stories have been subsequently reprinted in other anthologies.

A "White Girl, Fine Girl"

"White Girl, Fine Girl," Grau's first professionally published story, is set in Clayton County in an otherwise unidentified Southern state. Stanhope is the state capital, and Kilby, seven miles away, is the site of the "colored prison." Jayson Paul Evans, just released from the prison after serving most of a twenty year prison term for manslaughter, moves through the countryside to Stanhope to see Aggie, the widow of

Mannie, whom he had killed in a fight resulting from Mannie's finding
him and Aggie together. Entering the Pair-a-Dice Bar, Jayson meets
Joe, who has also been a lover of Aggie's but who prefers a peaceful
conversation to conflict. Jayson finds out that Aggie now has been
"born again" and has nothing to do with men, especially since her oldest girl was sired by Jayson at the time Mannie caught the two. As he
heads toward Aggie's house, the children (each with a different father)
throw stones and pieces of brick at Jayson—as they had earlier at Joe—
simply because he is walking down their street. As the children and
Aggie flee the house, Jayson, bloody from the onslaught of stones, ram-
pages through it and encounters his daughter. As Jayson leaves, satisfied, for the bar, the daughter follows him, evidently curious to know
her father, till he halfheartedly throws a stone after her and she leaves.
The story ends when Jayson enters a house to have sex with a white
woman, evidently a surrogate for the light-skinned Aggie.

The story is not a complicated one, except insofar as Aggie's various
lovers and their respective children need to be kept separate. Jayson's
time in prison, from his point of view, is to some extent Aggie's fault,
since her provocative nature led both him and Joe to have sexual relations with her. And Joe, although out of prison while Jayson has been
in, has fared no better with the independent Aggie, who wants nothing
to do with any man. Similarly, the stone-throwing incident with the
girls is paralleled with Jayson's almost leisurely tossing a stone at his
daughter; just as Aggie and her children, having "gotten religion,"
want nothing to do with him, so Jayson, in turn, wants nothing to do
with his daughter. And, finally, his going to a white woman is also
parallel to his attempting to go to Aggie, with the added irony of his
choosing a white woman rather than merely a light-skinned one; earlier, in the tavern, Joe had pointed to the white girl pictured on the Jax
beer poster and had advised Jayson to find one like her.

Further parallels are referred to earlier in the story: as Jayson leaves
the prison, he skips a stone across the river, almost to the other bank,
as if to suggest that although the other bank is close, it is still too far to
be reached easily, just as in prison the outside world was close enough
to touch, but was not available to Jayson. When he encounters two
small black boys in the woods, their immediate response is to pull a
knife, just as he had an ice-pick with Mannie, leading to his
imprisonment.

But the primary emphasis in the story is on "casting the first stone,"
on Jayson's sensing the need of avoiding retribution, even though

Aggie cannot do so. For Jayson, having spent many years in prison for killing a man, now has no desire to seek revenge against Aggie, only an urge to see her and the daughter he had sired by her but never seen, and thereafter to return to life as he had known it prior to prison.

Grau is especially effective with atmosphere in this story, but the plot is somewhat contrived, with parallels between separate incidents in the story and with biblical and mythic parallels being both ironic and too obvious: Jayson (Jason?) is cast out of the comfortable home he has known for many years (prison) and immediately heads for Pair-a-Dice (both Paradise and chance) to renew relations with Aggie, but ends up with forbidden fruit of another sort with a white woman.

B *"The Black Prince"*

"The Black Prince," originally published as "The Sound of Silver," is a successful blending of naturalistic detail with fablelike mystery, and with more than a few of the biblical echoes found in the other stories in this collection. The story opens with an epigraph, lines from Isaiah 14:12 that effectively indicate Grau's intention in the story: "How art thou fallen from heaven, O Lucifer, son of the morning!" For "The Black Prince" in this story is clearly identified with one with supernatural abilities and appeal, as well as the ability to seem to appear and disappear without warning.

Alberta Lucy, light-skinned beauty in the impoverished community in which the story takes place, is introduced throwing a stone, as in the previous story, but at birds, not people. And as she hears the sound of the birds, an added whistle is also heard, that of a man suddenly appearing from around a tree. When asked, he says he "just come straight out the morning" (42),[2] and tells Alberta her full name, even though she has never seen him previously. As he leaves without sound, she joins her friend Maggie Mary Evans to work in the fields. At lunch he appears to both girls, tells his name—Stanley Albert Thompson—and leaves, without even a depression in the pine needles and grass to indicate where he had been seated.

In time he joins the crowd at Willie's Bar and wins several fights in which he is involved. Willie, who makes corn liquor to sell in addition to running the bar, is also interested in Alberta, but can only watch as the two spend the silver that Albert seems never to run out of. In addition, Albert has a watch and ring—the only ones in the hamlet—worth as much as all the money seen in a year thereabouts. Indeed, when Alberta visits his shack (lit with candles instead of the more common lamps), he takes some wax from candle-drippings, rolls it around, and makes new silver coins until Alberta's dress pockets are full.

Thereafter they are inseparable at Willie's, even though the community is irreparably split because of a long-dormant feud that has arisen again, to some extent because of Stanley Albert's presence. Once a man named Pete Stokes shot at Stanley Albert but missed; a chase ensued in which the thick bushes "seemed to pull back and make way" (68) for him as he chased Pete, who was never seen again, dead or alive. The story ends with Willie's casting four silver bullets (from melting down the coins paid him by Stanley Albert) and shooting Stanley Albert dead-center in the chest. As he attempts to stand after being shot, Stanley Albert's eyes become two polished pieces of silver, and a black pool of blood forms on the floor. But he is not killed; he and Alberta disappear, and in the ten or so years following, many calamities occur, including Willie's dying when his barn burns. And thereafter the couple become part of a legend:

And kids sometimes think they hear the jingle of silver in Stanley Albert's pocket, or the sound of his watch. And when women talk—when there's been a miscarriage or a stillbirth—they remember and whisper together.

And they all wonder if that's not the sort of work they do, the two of them. Maybe so; maybe not. The people themselves are not too sure. They don't see them around any more. (70-71)

So the story ends—mysteriously, abruptly.

The mythical parallels in this story are obvious and require little comment. Stanley Albert evidently is a "fallen Angel," an angel of light, of the morning, one who, like Lucifer, comes to lead others to evil and/or death. Without pushing biblical echoes too far, one can see numerous ways in which this story relates to some of the same motifs found in the other stories in this collection, particularly the emphasis on a "prince of darkness" visiting earth with destruction and fire. Interestingly enough, one character with which the story begins, Maggie Mary, does not seem part of this motif (she is dropped by the middle of the story), even though her name is clearly a variation on Mary Magdalen.

Grau's powers of imagination and ability to evoke an atmosphere of mysterious uncertainty are at their best in this, the title story in this collection, even if the substance of the story is no more tangible than Stanley Albert's own presence. As evocative presence, the story excels; but whatever conflict there is in the story seems contrived and unequal. Indeed, one cannot help but identify more with Willie than with any other character in the tale, simply because he undergoes a more meaningful alteration because of the "prince" than does anyone else. After all, Alberta merely seems to have found her price in Stanley Albert, the highest bidder for her favors, while Willie's business and eventually his life are snuffed out by the actions resulting from the "black prince's" coming to his bar.

C "Miss Yellow Eyes"

"Miss Yellow Eyes," set in New Orleans during the Korean conflict, concerns two sisters, fourteen-year-old Celia and seventeen-year-old Lena, and two young men, the girls' older brother Pete and his friend Chris. The older girl had "eyes that were light brown with flecks of gold in them" (74), hence her nickname which serves as the story's title. The beautiful Lena, pursued by most of the other boys in high school, chooses Chris; both are fair-skinned Negroes, and both talk of "passing" for white by moving to Oregon. Pete, by contrast, is militantly black, and is active in a club dedicated to "better days" in the future. Chris and Lena are married, after which Chris is drafted, wounded in Korea, and killed in Japan. Pete's hand is amputated as a result of an accident on the railroad where he works as a switchman; embittered, he continues to comment about Chris' wishing to "pass." The story ends when Pete viciously attacks Chris as "dead and rotten," and Lena strikes him with their father's photograph.

But the essence of the story is more than the latent violence suggested by the events in the story. The two men's differing reactions to "color" is precisely the story's center, with a strong basis for this conclusion based on Grau's frequent awareness of sensory details. Lena and Chris, for example, are light enough to pass for white, and their eyes are also unlike the usual: Lena's eyes, as mentioned, are golden, and Chris' are blue. The all-black club Pete belongs to has a sign on the entrance saying "*White* entrance to *Rear*," a reversal of the usual segregationist pattern. Celia by mistake calls a white-owned cab for Lena, a cab painted orange; when the driver refuses to pick up "colored," she calls the right one, a cab painted black with gold stripes. On the way to the beach for some late-season wading, the four pass first the white beach, crowded with bathers, and eventually reach the "black" one, nearly deserted. Significantly, Celia notices that it was "all the one color" (93), all the same darkness until one saw white breakers and stars, as if to suggest the violence with which the story ends, in which one wishing to be "white" is killed in the darkness of war. And when Lena is told of Chris' death her eyes change in hue from golden to dark, dull brown.

This is almost a simplistic dichotomy between lighter and darker shadings of color, but it nonetheless works: the various shades of yellow or golden—light skin colorings for Lena and Chris, Lena's eyes, the "white" cab, and so on—suggest the world "out there," the white world, the world of freedom of movement and existence. And the darker hues, similarly, suggest the more constricted world of blackness. Even the "colored" cab, black with gold stripes, operates in a world exclusively black but with whiteness emphatically superimposed. And Pete, the more radical of the two men, is identified several times with redness, again almost simplistically, as when Lena hits his arm-stump and he insanely runs outside in agony.

Another level of meaning is suggested by Grau's repeated use of religiously symbolic names for her characters. Lena is short for Magdalena; she and her Chris (Christ), it seems, are both victims, to some extent, because of Pete (Peter): Pete's outburst at the story's end could constitute a "betrayal" of sorts, a betrayal of both his friend and his sister. The father had deserted the family years previously, we are told, and only the picture remains. But the picture itself had first been gotten out by the mother of the three siblings the night that Chris came to join them, almost as if an identification between the two is intended. And then Chris is killed, killed through dying for others. Finally, when Pete speaks disparagingly of Chris at the story's end, denying him, Lena hits his stub of an arm with the picture. Lena gasps, "Damn, damn, damn, damn," and Pete, running out in pain, screams, "Jesus, Jesus, Jesus, Jesus" (114–15)—whether as a mere exclamation or in reference to Chris, the reader isn't sure. But even the number of identical exclamations suggests a parallel between Lena's statement (damning her brother?) and Pete's reply.

"Miss Yellow Eyes" may be all too obvious because of the parallels cited, but it remains in any event a rather powerful account of the clash of convictions based on color.

D *"The Girl with the Flaxen Hair"*

Of all the stories in this collection, "The Girl with the Flaxen Hair" is the one with most of the quality of a fairy tale or myth. Lily, young daughter of the town dentist, notices new neighbors moving into the vacant house sharing the block with her own family's house, and soon discovers a beautiful yellow-haired girl her own age named Rose, and her parents, living there. Rose's father is found to be a mere barber, but her mother, daughter of a famous though dishonest politician else-where in the state, prefers to embellish the reality of the family with tales of grandeur and glory. Lily's father, a commonsensical dentist, is not taken in by Rose's mother, but Lily's mother finds her to be charm-ing. Rose's father leaves, ostensibly to study music in his native France, and the remaining members of the family carry on as if nothing is amiss.

Yet much is amiss, as Lily's father discovers early one winter morn-ing when he sees Rose sneaking out in the dark to steal coal from the piles in the railroad yard. The truth, then, is that though fiercely proud, the two remaining members of the family are impoverished. When spring comes, Rose continues her early-morning forays, and on one particular day, when the train schedule has been changed, she is struck and killed by a speeding passenger train. Her mother then leaves the town forever, and life in the town resumes its routine as it had been two years earlier.

Lily in time grows up, we are told in the last paragraph of the story, and as she matures she cannot always recall what her own father looked like, but she will always remember Rose and the almost legend-ary politician Rose and her mother had so often described, complete with shiny boots and a blue coat with silver buttons. Though she pre-sumably learns, as her father had told her, that the politician was a fake, the image she has of him and the "girl with the flaxen hair" will remain with her as long as she lives.

Much of the fairy-tale quality of the story, at least insofar as Lily is concerned, results from the fairly obvious comparison between the two girls. Lily, despite her name, is far from bland or pale, and her tomboy antics, even when she injures herself, do not noticeably alter her real-istic awareness of the life around her. Rose, though, is a far paler girl, and although she once endures a dental extraction without any sort of grimace or complaint, she does in reality reflect a less substantial, more

ethereal personality. It is almost as if Rose and her mother, by so completely living a lie and by so assiduously maintaining the facade of
respectable gentility, are less able to adapt to the realistic demands of
life than are Lily and her family, who matter-of-factly accept the com-
ings and goings of life. Hence when Rose is killed, the entire myth that
Lily had built up around Rose is embellished to the point of being
perpetual truth, with Rose's image a far more substantial one than the
relatively unclear one her own living father reflects. Even the story's
title resembles that found in a collection of fairy tales, such as those by
Hans Christian Andersen, and so we are not surprised when this golden
daughter of the morning dies, leaving the sorrowful neighbor girl to
embellish the reality with permanence.

E   *"The Bright Day"*

   Charlotte, married for only a year to Andrew, finds that she has also
inherited his older aunt and uncle, twins, as well as a perpetually drunk
cousin. She also finds, in the blisteringly hot summer in which the story
takes place, that she is part of a family scheme. An aged family member named Pamela, who has been away traveling around the world for
some thirty years, is returning home. Pamela is the legitimate heir to
her late sister's fortune, but Andrew and his aunt and uncle have con-
spired to take the money for themselves. And though Charlotte at first
intends to tell Pamela, she does nothing, for Andrew, firmly and persuasively, convinces her that it would be better that she do and say
nothing. The final paragraphs of the story, beginning with Charlotte's
saying, "I think we've used the money very practically" (162), tells of
how she and Andrew have used the money to build a house on a farm,
while Pamela lives off another, lesser annuity in a small house in town.
If Pamela suspects anything, she never says anything accusingly. But
Charlotte, though she found the price one she could not resist, still nur-
tures a residual conscience and hurries home after having tea with
Pamela, afraid that her "fairy mist castle" might have blown away,
broken in pieces the way a greenhouse was during a hailstorm
described early in the story.
   A slight story, this one too has something of the fairy-tale quality to
it, at least in part because of the epigraph to the story: "Finish, good
lady; the bright day is done, and we are for the dark." Wholly aside
from the relevance of the source for this epigraph, Shakespeare's
Antony and Cleopatra (V, ii, 192), in the story itself it has the sugges-

tive quality of indicating that this "good lady," Charlotte, though unable to escape the "bright day" and the perpetually burning heat, has in fact opted for the "dark," for a life of comfort rather than integrity, for a life of luxury based on a series of deceitful lies rather than the life of struggle required by following her original firm resolve and conscience. Little aside from their initials even implicitly relates Andrew and Charlotte to Antony and Cleopatra, unless one were to cite the luxury both women enjoy. Hence the title is ironic, for though the days continue to be hot beyond endurance, they cease to be bright, at least for Charlotte, as she grows older, becomes the mother of two children, and continues to betray the innocent Pamela. The story itself is rather obvious, offering little opportunity for analysis, and is one of the less memorable tales in the collection.

F *"Fever Flower"*

Differing from the other stories in this collection in that it concerns fairly sophisticated city dwellers, "Fever Flower" is a sensitive account of the tensions between Hugh and Katherine Fleming, divorced parents of three-year-old Maureen, and their respective lives apart from each other. Katherine, aged twenty-five, prepares to leave the house for her ex-husband's one-day-a-week visit with Maureen; the one detail about Katherine we are likely to remember, other than her loveliness, is the fact that "she was not quite human. She did not need anyone" (172). Hugh, though, has remarried and will be a father again shortly. Maureen, her room decorated by her mother as would be the room of a much older girl, becomes the focal point between the two parents, at least in part because neither really wants her very enthusiastically, Katherine because she is basically narcissistic, and Hugh because as a businessman he does not get as much return from supporting Maureen as the support costs him.

On this day together, Hugh and Maureen first play happily in the house with Hugh giving her her bath, something he rarely does, and then with the two of them going to the park for the day. While there, she takes him into the heavily humid conservatory where exotic plants that flourish in the heavy atmosphere—orchids in particular—saturate the air with their fragrance. Maureen, wearing an orchid pinafore, is clearly intended to appear one with the plants and the humid atmosphere. The flowers, we are told, "were forced to grow to gigantic size in half the time; they were beautiful and exotic and they did not last"

(176). To some extent this fits both Maureen and her mother, for both are beautiful and exotic, and the joy Hugh has experienced with both women in his life is doomed to diminish and eventually become extinguished. Taking Maureen home, Hugh finds that she does not want to take off her orchid dress, despite the overwhelmingly oppressive humidity.

It remains for Annie, the housekeeper, to best present a point of reference by which the others in the story can be evaluated. Deeply religious, Annie reads (in Paul's letter to the Galatians) that one should "Walk in the spirit and you shall not fulfill the lusts of the flesh. . . . The fruit of the spirit is joy." As Annie reflects on the passage, she sees both Hugh and Katherine burning in hell while she, Annie, takes Maureen by the hand to heaven.

Grau parenthetically tells of the future for each of the persons in the story, with none of them achieving anything close to happiness, and with Maureen herself going through three divorces before she settles down on the west coast; this is almost as if it were a prophetic utterance on Grau's part, based at least in part in Annie's self self-righteous fanaticism. One tends to sympathize with Hugh, who is better out of the marriage with Katherine than he would have been had the marriage continued, and with Maureen, who is only a child. Yet Hugh is fully as self-centered as his ex-wife (significantly, she demanded the divorce) in his seeing personal relationships in commercial terms, and Maureen is obviously growing up to be as spoiled and self-conscious of her beauty as her mother had been.

Maureen is the "fever flower" of the story's title, the orchid growing too fast in the heavy atmosphere of the hothouse environment; unable to survive in the "normal" outside atmosphere, she, like the flower, thrives in the unnatural aura of high humidity, lush attention, and careful nurturing. Though Maureen has a fever at the story's end, this, it seems to me, is merely a physiological means of drawing the comparison even more tightly between the child and the greenhouse plants she had seen that afternoon. Were it not for Grau's parenthetic comment about Maureen's subsequent life, we would surely think, from the story's last lines—"She did not turn again: she had stopped crying. And lay there, beautiful and burning" (180)—that she, like the orchids, would soon die, burned out before normal maturity has even occurred. Such, however, is not the case; Maureen like her mother is destined to be a person who could completely cut herself off from the past. Just as

Katherine had never seen Hugh once they were divorced, so one can deduce that Maureen, as she grows up, will also cut herself off from her parents, as they—Katherine because of her narcissism, Hugh because of his new family—occupy less and less of Maureen's life.

Although not a complicated story, "Fever Flower" does work rather well on the levels of both the realistic story and the symbolic underpinnings, even though a more experienced writer would have been able to intertwine the two more subtly than Grau did at the time the story was published. Still, it remains one of the more effectively realized of the tales in this collection.

G "The Way of a Man"

Although the title of "The Way of a Man" is taken from the well-known passage in Proverbs 30:18–19, there is little in this tale to do "with a maid." Instead, Grau's concern is with the development of a boy into a man, the movement from innocence to initiation into a degree of maturity. (Ironically, an autobiographical volume by Grau's husband, as mentioned in the first chapter, also carries the title *The Way of a Man*.) But this initiation does not result in genuine responsibility so much as in frantic running away from responsibility.

Set on a Louisiana bayou, the story concerns William, born to a youthful mother and an old father. At birth he was ignored by both parents: his mother because she had married in expectations of wealth and without, she thought, any likelihood of pregnancy; and his father because he was old and seemingly uninvolved in much of life. His mother kept him till he was two, then his father till he was seven. Since he grew quickly, he had a man's body without the corresponding man's perspective by the time he was in his teens, and much of the story relates to this inconsistency. By seventeen he had his own woman and had spent time at a reform school. But he was proud of being a man, even in one situation, in the reform school, when mere daydreaming about a circus was the primary reason why he did not run away; the chaplain's comment that he had "behaved like a man" (189) is merely the first such ironic usage of the term in the story.

Visiting his father for the first time in years, William goes with him out to fish. The two see an overturned skiff, which William insists is his; when they find the body of a young white girl, William's manliness does not extend even to being able to look at her body. It is up to the old man to dispose of the corpse, which he does through dumping it in the deeper part of the bayou. "A man's got no call to do some things iffen he don't want to" (199), is William's halfhearted reply, along with such added comments as "A man can take what he wants" (200). But the father keeps the skiff, since William is wary of taking that which belongs to the dead.

William subsequently goes to his mother's house again. Some four months later his woman tells him that the police are looking for him, which he suspects is because he has hidden a parcel of marijuana under his bed. Though he says "A man got no call to be afraid" (203), he is in fact terrified of being caught, even if he has done nothing to warrant such fear. Attempting to run away, he ends up at his father's house, where is is taunted at supposedly being a man but in reality being frightened. Furious, he strikes out at his father, killing him; he ransacks the house, finding a few silver dollars, justifying his actions in terms of manliness. The story ends with William's wrapping himself up in a heavy quilt against the night fog, planning to escape to New Orleans the following morning.

As an exercise in deluded futility, the story works quite well. William's conflict with both parents is made vividly real, and his misguided efforts to appear grown-up are seen in the contrasting deaths—the young white girl, and his father. Yet the story ends with William shivering in the dark, having to live with the things he has done. Interestingly, motive is at no time a factor in any of William's actions: he wants the skiff merely as a possession until he discovers it belongs to the dead; he does not intend to kill his father, but does so and then tries to escape. Though the reader is not told, it seems inevitable that escape is impossible, that William's "way of a man" is little more than a shadow of real manliness, simply because he does not take upon himself any responsibility for his actions. Things occur; he responds to situations simply on a visceral level, without any foresight or afterthought. As we are told, "Sometimes he did not intend to, but things came to him and he did them" (211).

The story, like others in this collection concerned with illiterate blacks in the Gulf Coast setting favored by Grau, is especially effective because of the skill with which atmosphere is captured. One can feel particularly well in this story the dense fog and the corresponding moral fog William is in, just as one can sense his total alienation from society as a result of his dispossession by both parents. And, despite the inevitability of the story's ending, one still cannot help but feel the agony of being in William's situation. All in all, it is a successful story, though more on a consistently realistic level than most of the others in the collection.

H *"One Summer"*

"One Summer" is considerably more atmospheric than most of Grau's stories in that the entire world in the story is under thunderheads that threaten imminently to drench and even kill some of those whose lives are wholly dependent upon the weather. The two main movements of the story—the sudden coming-of-age of a young man and the death of his grandfather—are almost ignored in the engulfing humidity and heaviness of the threatening weather. In this respect, the story resembles Grau's *The Hard Blue Sky*, in which the characters perpetually await the tropical storms that we know will wipe out all they have built up in a lifetime. But the story is more subtle in that a very small number of characters, really, are focused on: MacDonald "Mac" Addams, from whose point of view the story is told; Eunice Herbert, his girl, with whom moments of teenage passion are stolen; his parents, who for the first time become fully human for Mac. There are in addition a number of older folk, contemporaries of the dead man, who reminisce endlessly about the past, and the black servants, whose feelings are almost totally ignored by the whites at the wake. Mac points out in the opening line of the story that "You forget most things, don't you?" (213). And it is true that forgetfulness blots out most memories, particularly the unpleasant ones. But the summer in which the story takes place is eventful for him.

In one sense, the ending of one person's life becomes the start of another's. Mac and Eunice steal kisses and embraces, even as the grandfather is dying, suggesting the rising of mature responses, emotional and physical, in Mac as circumstances force him to accept adult relationships without his desiring them. As his mother awaits his father at his dead grandfather's house, Mac notices for the first time, in three successive afterthoughts, that he had never thought of his mother as having nice legs before, of having as good a figure as Eunice, and of having a "fuzz of yellow hair all up her leg" (227). This is not mere displaced sexuality; rather, it is that Mac realizes, with death for the first time facing him personally, that in time his parents too will die and that he will wait for the mortician with his own son beside him. For the first time Mac sees his mother as a woman rather than merely as a maternal figure. His father notes that "he's almost a man" (229), a considerably more mature man, in fact, than the protagonist in "The Way of a Man."

The ephemeral nature of life impresses Mac in another way too. His nightly ritual for two months has been to sneak across the street to Eunice's house and then to spend a few choice moments in her backyard talking and kissing before retiring. At the wake for his grandfather, Mac is brought a Coke by Eunice, but nothing remains of the bearer: "She was gone then. And there was only the Coke taste in my mouth to remind me that she had been there. And that was gone soon, and there was just the dust taste. And there wasn't a trace of her. I just couldn't believe that she had been there . . . it was funny, the way things were beginning not to seem real" (231–32). And as the wake continues, Mac is sent home by his father, but Mac does not at first understand why his father wishes to be alone; but before the evening is over, he, too, wishes solitude, even from Eunice. He reminisces about his last time with his grandfather two days earlier, and the fishing expedition they went on, an expedition on which the old man did not cast out his line, instead preferring simply to wait, to be left alone:

The fear of dying . . . the fear that grows until at last it separates you from the people you know: the dusty-eyed old people who want to be left alone, who go off alone and wait. Who fish without a line.
    One day I'll be that afraid. . . . All of a sudden I knew that. Knew that for the first time, I'll be old and afraid. (252–53)

And as the story ends, Mac, alone, leaned "back against the sharp thorns of the hedge. And listened" (255).

The story is quite affecting, and in its capturing of the moment in adolescence when a youth looks back at carefree youth and inevitable death simultaneously, it resembles other classic stories on this theme, such as Sherwood Anderson's "Sophistication." For Mac has achieved a degree of maturity in this one evening, symbolized by the "sir" his grandfather's black servant uses for the first time with him. Never again will he be the same, nor will his relationships with others, especially Eunice, be quite the same. Simply as a story, however, this tale is too involved and elaborate for the relatively simple point being made, for one cannot help but feel that most young adolescents have a greater gut-level understanding of death than Mac reflects in much of the story.

I "*Joshua*"

The last story in the collection, "Joshua," concerns an eleven-year-old Cajun boy living on the Gulf Coast below New Orleans in an isolated area scarcely touched by the passing events of history. More than any other story in this collection, however, topical references are significant: the story is set in early World War II, when German U-boats were located in the gulf near Louisiana, and U-boats figure in the story.

Joshua Samuel Watkin lives with his parents; his father, a sometime fisherman, is hesitant to go out to the gulf because the boat of a fellow fisherman had been blown up by a U-boat, with the man piloting the boat killed. But Joshua needs a winter coat, for the winter rains are incessantly saturating everything to the core. And the family needs food, too. His father preferring to stay drunk the entire day, Joshua sets out with only another young boy to bring home the food that is needed. The threat of German invaders is lessened by the knowledge that one U-boat was blown up by shore patrol vessels. As the two boys check the various fishing lines strung out in the bayou, Joshua glimpses a slot of blue, the one color not indigenous to the swamp. He investigates, finds it to be the body of a German (presumably blown up in the submarine), removes the jacket from the body, and returns home.

Joshua is as frightened as his father of the menace awaiting anyone venturing out into the waters, but he still goes; his reason, as we are told, is that "there was something he had to prove" (287). Nazis, snakes, and alligators are no threat when he sees something he wants. The story is thus one more exploration of youth proving itself to be courageous and mature; as such, it is not so effective or impressive as "One Summer" or "The Way of a Man," but it is a captivating story simply because Joshua, like his biblical namesake, is not easily dissuaded by overwhelming forces. But the chief force he has to contend with is not the snakes or the U-boats or anything else animate or man-made; it is, rather, the totally pervasive, suffocatingly humid atmosphere of the Gulf Coast winter, a season with little freezing temperatures but with persistent, drenching rains. The weather affects others by enabling them to justify their inertia, as with Joshua's father, or to use arthritis as a means to stay close to a warm fire, as with the father of the boy who accompanies Joshua. In either case, Joshua proves himself a "man" in that he gets food, he gets the jacket he needs, he ventures out into waters that others temporarily shun, and he approaches the body of a dead German when others merely talk about the threat "out there."

II   The Wind Shifting West

Given the highly favorable critical reception of *The Black Prince and Other Stories* and the frequent appearance in magazines of subsequent stories by Grau, it was naturally only a matter of time till an additional collection was published. Yet when *The Wind Shifting West* appeared nineteen years after the earlier collection, the critical reaction was decidedly antagonistic. While the book is not the "unmitigated disaster"[3] that it was called by a reviewer in the *Washington Post*, it was also surely not so consistently rewarding as the earlier collection. And while some of the stories are sharply evocative and memorable, most are merely competent, lacking much emotional drive and substance, and a few are simply disappointing. Two of the stories are early draft versions of works subsequently expanded and published as novels: "The Patriarch" is a previously unpublished synopsis of *Evidence of Love*, already discussed, and "Stanley" is an early version of portions of *The Condor Passes*, also discussed above. The remaining sixteen stories, all but two of which originally appeared in periodical form, deal to a great extent with isolation and displacement, especially concerning women, and one of the stories, a very successful one, is Grau's only published effort at creating an end-of-the-world atmosphere.

A   *"The Wind Shifting West"*

The title story in this collection is about Caroline Edwards, a reluctant sailor with her husband Robert on his new boat. A "great sailor," he is smoothly competent, even further alienating and isolating her from the life he and their small daughter enjoy. So, while her family goes out sailing, she joins the others at the family reunion. When word comes that Robert has broken his mast through carelessness, she goes with her sister's husband Giles to the rescue. Giles, though, goes the long way, to a deserted cove, where he seduces Caroline before going after Robert. Caroline, dissatisfied after the experience, acknowledges that there is not much left after the act, just some weed on the anchor and some salt dried on their skin, and she is bothered by the absence of feeling. Just as her husband was too occupied with his boat to notice her as a person, so her brother-in-law is too intent on his goal to detect the degree of unhappiness she feels.

A slick, deft story, "The Wind Shifting West" is an adequate though undistinguished account of the despair beyond words a person may feel when he feels completely alone, even while in the presence of many other people. Caroline finds that she has nothing to say at the family reunion other than small talk about how this person has grown since last year, or how that person has changed. In a vigorous family like Robert's, Caroline's pale, untanned appearance is distinctly out of place. Hence even seduction offers the potential of being noticed, though here too she is disappointed because of Giles' self-assured manner and his too-confident air of superiority, even in knowing that she will give in to his seductive approach. But after the sexual act, Caroline feels neither more fulfilled nor more emotionally moved, neither guilty nor intrigued, by the encounter; she remains as alone as before.

B *"The Householder"*

Originally published as "The Burglar," the change of title reflects a more accurate focus in the story. Also a domestic tale about the isolation experienced by a woman presumably surrounded by love, this story concerns a married couple (Harry and Nora) awakened in the middle of the night by unmistakable sounds of burglars stealthily entering their house. Nearsighted without his glasses, Harry can barely see one of the burglars escaping over a fence outside. Nonetheless he shoots in the direction of the man, with the other burglar escaping safely. When the police come, they find the burglar, dead, lying by the fence, the result of what the police term a "lucky shot." Though the night is almost over, they consider going back to sleep as a means of forgetting what has happened, but neither of them, particularly Nora, can ignore the killing, even though Harry, as a "householder," had the right to protect his home and family. It is, in fact, merely the reality of death and its impact on their domestic bliss that comprises the point of the story, an uncomplicated and fairly obvious tale.

C *"Homecoming"*

A considerably more successful story, "Homecoming" is, as a *New York Times* critic termed it, a "bitter blow at Southern sentimentality and love of ritual."[4] A nineteen-year-old boy whom the protagonist, Susan, barely knew has been killed in Vietnam, and the occasion of his death leads her relatives to treat the occasion as a major death in the family. Since her father had also been killed in war, her mother especially considers the death an occasion for wholesale mourning. Susan is not at all upset, but the manner in which her mother and their friends exaggerate the closeness of the two teenagers—her mother constantly reminds her that the two would have gotten married, with her fervent denials proving useless—is such as to cause Susan to retreat into her own room, even further reinforcing the others' conviction that she is bereaved. Susan then realizes that she too "is obeying a set of rules" (53)[5] and that the boy's being dead really will not change anything for her, despite all that her mother is saying. In other words, she can see her mother's desperate attempts to force sympathy on her as a way to have a "good time," as a major incident in the humdrum life her mother experiences. The story ends with Susan whispering to the dead boy, "Good-by, you poor bastard" (54), as she rejoins the others gathered to commisserate.

Grau's tone is especially good in this story, for it would not have taken much for a touch of complete cynicism to enter in, with the mother made comical instead of pathetic or Susan hard-boiled instead of aloof. As it is, Susan remains as alone as she had been previously, but she has reached a level of understanding she had not had, not even when she first heard of the boy's death. For now she realizes *why* her mother reacts as she does, why death is an occasion for people to come together to share the experience. And even if in this case the emotional depth of the "loss" is radically overestimated, the occasion still serves as a form of ceremony by which sharing can occur.

Hence in joining the people in her house at the story's end, Susan reflects a degree of maturity her earlier rebelling against her mother's excited planning did not reflect. It is a convincing story, one that makes a serious point without resorting to the extremes of either comic ridicule or grotesque caricature. And just as Susan can now understand her mother, so we too can understand a bit better the emotion of personal and communal reaction to death.

D   *"The Beach Party"*

Another account of death as experienced by the young, who least expect the reality of death to impinge upon their daily routine, "The

Beach Party" tells of Frieda, teenage "little sister" to Everett who, with his own friends, are having a party to which she was reluctantly brought along. Even though one of Everett's friends, John, pays attention to her and begins to hold her, she still feels as if she does not belong there. She walks away and notices a group of skin-divers some distance away. Later, after they eat, word comes that one of the skin-divers failed to return. Everett and the others go to try to find his body, and when they drag it back to shore, Frieda notices one of the dead youth's friends sitting, numbed and in shock. After the police take away the body, everyone is excited and gradually leaves the beach—leaving Frieda there, no one having noticed that she was not in any of the cars.

Sitting alone, Frieda wishes that she could have talked with the shocked survivor and told him that death is a normal part of the routine of life. She wonders why the youth's death does not bother her more than it does, no more than the death of lobsters or other animals, "than the sharp smell of a man's sweat, or the angular pressure of another body" (81). But how "useless" it all is, she realizes, even though such a "surge of protection" is a normal part, along with ovulation, of her being female. And as she leaves the beach for the long walk home, the sound of her radio serves as a small form of protection itself, with her safely "inside its tinny shell" (82).

As with "Homecoming," this story is an account of a young woman's discovering the subtle reality of death. And although one might wish to have "The Beach Party" developed at greater length (as, for example, in allowing us to see more of what leads Frieda to her present conviction other than the skin-diver's death), it is a convincing little tale of emotional desolation combined with certainty about Frieda's own subsequent handling of emotional crises such as death.

E *"Three"*

A very fine account of the effects of death upon a sensitive soul, "Three" tells of Ann Richards, whose husband Jerry had been killed in Vietnam more than two years previously, and who cannot escape Jerry's constant presence wherever she might be, just across the room or down the block when she is walking. In short, she is disturbed and obsessed by the reality of Jerry long after he ceases to live. Hence when Ted patiently, slowly begins to date her and fall in love with her, she gradually finds that she can exist without Jerry's constant presence. When she and Ted first make love, her apartment is "perfectly silent with a church-like emptiness" (94), without Jerry. She and Ted have to separate for a while, and Jerry "returns" and even "speaks" to her, coming closer to her than he had ever done before and saying that he would probably always be with her. After Ted returns, the couple make frantic love, and she again notices that Jerry's apparition is standing by the door.

Following her marriage to Ted and the return from their honeymoon, she again senses that Jerry is still there:

> *I'm so glad, Jerry*, she said silently, because it would only hurt Ted's feelings to hear. *You're not angry about Ted? You won't leave because there are three of us now?*
>
> Jerry went on smiling his kindest, most radiant smile. The edges of his figure shivered and sparkled with points of light. *Not this time. Not again. I'll be here*, he said, *I'll be here.* (99)

And as Ted enters the room, she says, "Come see, just come see": "The room shimmered and glowed all around her as she slipped her arm through his and led him into the living room to meet her husband" (99).

Clearly a case of extreme obsession, but more than a case of a woman having a love divided between her dead husband and her present one, this story presents an emotionally complex situation and attempts to show how the relatively mature reaction to death found in earlier stories in the collection—such as "Homecoming" and "The Beach Party"—completely passes Ann Richards by. She so consistently refuses to allow Jerry to "die" that he becomes more real than when he was living. All Ted amounts to is a physical surrogate for the ethereal Jerry, though he does not realize it this early in the marriage.

And Ann herself, by refusing to allow the dead to stay dead, is unconsciously creating another kind of death between her living husband and herself. For the threesome that she now envisions their having is obviously an untenable situation for a normal marriage, and only her adjustment to "reality" will alter the situation in any meaningful manner, for Jerry will no doubt stay just as she recalls him, youthful and handsome, while she and Ted change with the passing of time. This is, no doubt, a pathetic situation, but Grau handles it quite well. The story is convincing and touching, with the reader feeling sympathy for Ann, of course, and perhaps even more for Ted, the innocent participant in the three-way marriage.

F *"The Long Afternoon"*

Neither the title "The Long Afternoon" nor the story's original publication title, "The Longest Day," fully fits this account of a grumpy malcontent of an eleven-year-old girl who simply cannot be pleased. Recuperating from an appendectomy, Patsy knows she has been spoiled, and on a hot, muggy day, forbidden to move too strenuously, she is simply, wilfully bored. Hence anything to break the monotony and tedium is appealing, such as saying aloud in front of two delivery men, "I got to get a bigger bra" (103). And so Patsy irritates her big brother, teases a smaller child, anything to be noticed, including climbing up to a tree house—expressly forbidden because of her stitches—at the story's end: "'I won't ever come down,' she whispered. The sound startled her, so she went on talking to herself silently. 'I'll live up here. Until I get old and die. I'll stay until I get old and older and die'" (114). And then she fights against the tears that start to flow.

An uncomplicated and not particularly rewarding story, "The Long Afternoon" is more of a mere anecdote than a fully developed narrative about a moderately interesting human. Most readers will doubtless feel that Patsy is less than sympathetic and even less of a substantial character around whom to build a story. For she is limited at the story's beginning to the fairly trite category of "spoiled child," nothing she does thereafter alters this label in the slightest, and nothing she experiences in her tedious short life warrants any sympathy whatever; it is highly unlikely that the "traumatic" recuperation she must endure will alter her life in any manner whatsoever.

G *"The Land and the Water"*

Another story about sailing, "The Land and the Water" (originally titled "The Reach of Fog"), is also another account of death in the water. The speaker in the story, a young girl, and her slightly younger sister are spending the day scraping the family boat's hull when word comes that three other teenagers, older than the speaker, have been lost in a fog, though only one body has been recovered. As in "The Beach Party," the effects of the deaths on the protagonist constitute the focus of the story, but unlike the other story, this one does not allow us to see that the protagonist has gained anything from the experience. She contemplates what "it must be like to be dead and cold and down in the sand and mud with the eel grass brushing you and the crabs bumping you" (124–25) as she stands looking out over the water. Her mother's reaction, when the girl runs back into the house, is merely one of telling her to take off her wet garments. But to the girl, there was something more than the dew and the fog out there, "something that had reached for me, and missed. Something that was wet, that had come from the water, something that had splashed me as it went past" (125).

Yet nothing in the story itself, nothing in what the girl has experienced or pondered, convinces us that she has experienced anything more than a gut-level fear of drowning as a result of the news of the other young people's deaths. If the fog indeed has any "reach" at all, it seems merely sufficient to reach to this girl's adrenalin glands as she fearfully runs back into the warmth and security of her mother's kitchen; her mother's calm, complacent acceptance of the events of the day and the smell of frying bacon are more persuasive than the girl's frenetic reaction to the world of nature, even if that world sometimes brings with it the fact of death.

H   *"The Last Gas Station"*

Of all of Grau's fiction, long as well as short, this is evidently her one foray into the realm of the apocalyptic, into the kind of "end-of-the-world" fiction so often identified with such forms of fiction as speculative or science fiction. And even though the setting is the same one used so often in Grau's earlier work, a small bayou town below New Orleans in the Mississippi delta region, the very combination of the setting with the events in the story combine to make this an extremely effective tale, surely one of her stories that deserves far wider circulation.

The story, in brief, is of a family of a father and four boys who operate a run-down gas station on a four-lane highway heading straight to the South. Indeed, the highway becomes a kind of deity to the narrator, the youngest boy in the family, not only because the family cat had been killed on the road, but even more because, as a continually living entity, the highway seems to breathe. The family gradually diminishes in number as first Bruce leaves, then the father dies, Mark leaves, and then there are just Joe, the eldest, and the narrator, the youngest, left.

As Mark leaves, after a fight with Joe, he says, "Cain killed Abel. The end of the world is coming" (132), and this is indeed what seems to occur. At first there was too much traffic on the highway, all heading South (i.e., toward the gulf), with everyone wanting gasoline. When the station's tanks are depleted, the two surviving boys notice the great number of cars abandoned alongside the highway, then the highway itself closed as a result of a massive pile-up, and then no traffic at all. As Joe, still not knowing what has caused the changes in traffic past the station, decides that they too will leave, the narrator runs away and hides out of fear of Joe's anger and instability, until Joe too leaves, at which time the narrator returns to the empty station. But there is no more electricity, just total silence, not a single thing moving in any direction. And as the story ends, the narrator knows what he will do when the next car passes—if there is ever again another car or anything else moving in the world.

Many stories, of course, have been written about the "last days," the apocalyptic day when life will cease because of one catastrophe or another. Whether man-made or natural, the "end of the world" concept carries with it an inherent fear for many civilized people because of its promise of total disruption of the smooth, normal way civilized life is expected to function. An account of the end of life in a futuristic society has one effect upon us, and a realistic account of such cessation of life in a major urban setting quite a different one. Yet it remains true that the most fearful accounts of the final great cataclysm are those seen from the perspective of a rural setting. As with Walter Van Tilburg Clark's classic tale, "The Portable Phonograph," we realize that if the effects of the conflagration are so intense here in the hinterland, what must it have been like in urban centers?

In "The Last Gas Station," moreover, we experience these final days not through the eyes of relatively sophisticated observers, but through the eyes of a young, presumably uneducated boy who has had no contact with the outside world through any of the various forms of communication, not even any contact with others outside his family of similarly unlettered males. On one level, the story may seem to deal with a mere extreme form of sibling rivalry, as first one brother and then another flee. But Mark's comment about Cain and Abel may be nearer the point, for the story does have an aura of biblical doom, as if the world is coming to an end, with no place left to escape to, and with no survivors. And the setting, similar to one used by Grau many times in more conventional stories to establish a sense of place or mood, here serves all the more to heighten the horrors of what must be "out there," out where the protagonist cannot see but where he would like to be, just so he could know what has happened. One has not the slightest expectation of the events in this story when he begins to read it, for it seems like merely one more variation upon a familiar, even trite, theme. But Grau's accomplishment in the story is a fine one, to a great extent because of the very understated, calm manner in which apocalyptic horror is suggested, not shown directly.

I *"The Thieves"*

This story, originally entitled "The Man Below," is set in the French Quarter of New Orleans; Carrie heads toward a bar where she usually meets Steve. Growing old without the security of marriage she feels she needs, she waits for Steve to propose, but he prefers to come to her apartment whenever he feels like it and to meet her in the bar instead of taking her someplace more desirable. In a word, she has been passed by and now has few alternatives other than to do as Steve asks. After forty years of having lived in the United States, her parents had returned to Sicily, their homeland. and she had never followed. Her life, in brief, has little in it that is intrinsically interesting or exciting or secure, and Steve adds little to it, especially little in promise for the future.

Late one night she hears noises outside her apartment window and sees police with flashlights going from roof to roof looking for a burglar, whom she sees below her in the yard behind her house. From her perspective she sees that he is trying to find some way of getting over a wall to freedom. She whispers the way to the burglar, and he escapes successfully. But Steve, even at this hour, calls to come over, and she thinks of the lines from Marlowe's "The Passionate Shepherd to His Love": "Come live with me and be my love, / And we will all the pleasures prove." But when Steve comes, it is obvious that he wants to tell her that he will possibly be marrying someone else, a friend of his parents' family; when Carrie asks him directly, though, he cannot quite acknowledge that he will be getting married. Evidently he wishes both to maintain his relationship with Carrie whenever he wishes and to have the permanence and security of marriage to someone else. Suddenly tired of the entire routine, Carrie says, "Go home, little boy," and she realizes that "the silence was no emptier" after he left "than it had been with him there" (147).

Another tale of solitude and the effects of isolation upon a sensitive woman, this story shows how Carrie realizes that by helping the burglar to escape she has broken out against the conventional ways of thinking and behaving that she has had in her relationship with Steve. Now she has gone beyond the point where they have been in their relationship, gone "over the wall" like the burglar, and she sees how empty both their lives are. She thinks: "If I had a wall I could climb over it, but I don't even have a wall. I don't have anything at all" (147). Since Steve is in a sense the "wall" she must get over for her to experience anything remotely like freedom, she knows she must say "goodbye" to him if she is to maintain anything valid in her life.

Although this may seem a particularly poignant story because of Carrie's lack of fulfillment, in a sense it is an optimistic tale simply because she has moved beyond the point where she needs a man for her own life's fulfillment. Even if there is nothing "out there," beyond the "wall" she is climbing to escape the humdrum life with Steve, this would still be better than to continue as she has. Ironically, the original title for the story seems to fit better even though it appears at first glance to apply more to the escaping burglar than to anyone else. For "The Man Below" could apply just as validly to Steve as to the burglar, whereas "The Thieves" seems to fit none of the characters very well. Carrie has made her stand as a result of the experiences she has gone through with the burglar, and, live or die, she will henceforth have to find out for herself what exists on the other side of the "wall." The story is effective, all in all, and Grau's understated handling of the theme, especially the parallels to the Marlowe allusion, is good.

J *"The Other Way"*

Unlike most of the stories in this collection, which are not explicitly about life in the South, "The Other Way" is closely tied in with topical situations, in this case with enforced school desegregation in the 1950s and 1960s. A small black girl named Sandra Lee comes home to her Cajun-French-speaking relatives and acts moodily enough for them to know that something had happened in school that day. After interrogation, she reluctantly acknowledges that the white children, those who had been attending the school for years, will not sit by her during lunch, so she says she will not go back to that school. But, she is told, "you going tomorrow and all the days after. And when you come home in the evening, you are going to tell us what kind of a day you had, and what you did at lunchtime, and all that you learned" (153)—in other words, how well she, a scholarship student, put in a normal day in the strange white school. The story ends with Sandra Lee leaving through the front door (significantly, she had slunk unhappily through the kitchen door earlier), merely going out for a bottle of milk but knowing as well that she represents all her people and that she must act accordingly: "she felt the pressure of her people behind her, pushing her, cutting off her tears" (154). When she returns with the milk, her mother asks again, "How was school?" and Sandra Lee replies, "It was fine" (154). In other words, her perspective has changed because of those few minutes' talk at home a little earlier, and this changed attitude will henceforth enable her to do what is necessary in going to school each day.

An uncomplicated story, this makes a valid point and again deals with an isolated female, but it requires no extensive explication simply because it seems to fit a topical rather than an artistic framework. That is, the sociological point in the story is well taken, but there is nothing especially profound or original in the technique used to make the point.

K   *"The Man Outside"*

By contrast, this story deals with poor whites, with a family of a mother with eleven children and no husband living in the deep South, the father having decided that he wished to live by himself in the woods. Eventually the father in the family moves away completely, and in time a hard-working lumber-mill employee named Benton moves in and marries the mother, gets the farm working again, restores the family to a higher level of prosperity than they had known for years, and establishes a pattern of happiness in the home. The narrator, by this time nearly finished with his schooling, tells one day of seeing a man standing outside in the road staring at the house. "Make him go," his mother says, and Mr. Benton does so. Afterward, the boys ask who the man was, with the reply, "A tramp." But the mother has been affected by the sight, and after her eyes come "back to normal," Benton sits down, "solidly, so that he looked a part" (169) of his chair—and the home—in a way he had not looked previously. The boys did not ask about the tramp after that, not even years later, after Benton was dead and their mother an old lady rocking on the porch.

The reader, though, knows that the tramp is presumably the boys' shiftless father returned from years of tramping, expecting to find a welcome as years before, and completely rejected by the secure pattern of life his former family now enjoys. So obvious is this conclusion, in fact, that we are a little astonished that the narrator does not think of it, nor that no one else in the family thinks, then or in the later years, of mentioning the point. It is difficult to say whether "The Man Outside" or the story's original title, "Stranger at the Window," fits better, because in either case we know long before the end of the story what Grau's point is.

L "Sea Change"

Another woman suffering from the death of her husband is the subject of "Sea Change," but in this case the husband, a skilled pilot, has evidently been killed in the Vietnam war. His widow watches plane after plane leaving the large airport near her home, convinced that one of them would be his; she is evidently unable to accept the fact of his death, so by watching plane after plane taking off and landing safely, she can fantasize that he is still alive. But this one time, as she is leaving the observation deck, she nearly faints, and a man in blue uniform— we find out that he, too, is a pilot, having just brought a plane in safely—helps her, first with water, then with coffee, then with Scotch. Her hysteria over, she now knows that "everything was slowing down, . . . and there would be a quiet time. A perfectly still minute" (180). Later—evidently after she and the pilot have spent some private time together—time does end for her, and she tries to see (evidently one in a long line of such mental efforts) where her husband died, on a beach in Vietnam. She sees his body, sees him move and live again, and, smiling, starts to chuckle. The pilot who befriended her asks why she is laughing, and she replies, "Because there wasn't anything left. And he came back" (181).

This woman's isolation, unlike that experienced by some of the women in other stories in this collection, is resolvable through the intervention of another man. Her fantasy about seeing her dead husband's body, evidently a repeated pattern, ends for good when he appears to come back to life. In saying "there was nothing left," she clearly suggests both that his body was completely gone in the Vietnam affair and that his presence (unlike that of Ann Richards' husband in "Three") will no longer haunt her. And his "coming back" seems to suggest that the new pilot (who says, not too persuasively, that he has a wife and children in Cleveland) will now take the place, in all ways, of her husband. Whether or not anything permanent or secure occurs in her relationship with the new pilot, the ominous presence of the husband has now been exorcised. One tends to believe that her isolation is now at an end and that the pilot, knowingly or not, has performed a kind of therapy in his thoughtful ministrations to her. An effective story, this seems to suggest a more hopeful approach to isolation than do some of Grau's other stories on this point.

M   *"Pillow of Stone"*

This story is a return to the Gulf Coast islands south of New Orleans that served as the setting of Grau's first novel, *The Hard Blue Sky;* indeed, the central character, Ann Marie Landry, has the same family name as Annie Landry in that novel, but aside from the similarity of names, there seems to be no connection between the two characters. Ann Marie Landry lives with her husband Raoul on an island, and, again as in Grau's first novel, a storm is approaching. But storm or no storm, and pregnancy or no pregnancy, Ann Marie must go to the mainland because her father has died and she must join the rest of her family at his bedside. The only means of getting to the mainland, since all the island's boats are gone because of the imminent storm, is an old sloop a resident won in a poker game. So she and Raoul take the sloop and head carefully through the treacherous shoals for the mainland. Eventually arriving, she walks laboriously up the path to the house, smiling triumphantly.

One can speculate about possible meanings to this story, with the title itself suggesting a gravestone, on the one hand, and with Ann Marie's unborn child serving as a potential life to balance the death of her father. But the more obvious source for the title of the story is the account of Jacob and Esau's enmity and Jacob's dream of a ladder reaching to the heavens, with God telling Jacob that his "seed shall be as the dust of the earth" as he lay with his head on a pillow made of stones (Genesis 28: 1–15, especially verse 11); there would be little reason to use this source for the title of the story were we not to see Ann Marie as the progenitor, like Jacob, of a line of "blessed" descendants. It is not a complicated story, since it seems primarily to suggest the life-force that continues, in the presence even of death as well, and the family tradition that requires Ann Marie to return to her home no matter how difficult the way might be, even through a storm.

N "*Eight O'Clock One Morning*"

A family of white children prepare for the first day of school, school that is now integrated by court order. Carrie, the narrator, has to get her younger brother, starting kindergarten that morning, down to breakfast. But her father, going out and seeing troublemakers gathered near the school, tells his wife to keep the children home that day, first day or no first day. Even Carrie's boyfriend, who telephones, plans to stay out of school that day, in his case evidently to add to the trouble. Toughs wearing black leather jackets pass by the house, but no one knows them. "White niggers," the father calls them, "spoiling for trouble" (194), and he is proved correct when they start to throw objects at a passing bus. A diaper-service truck, driven by a black man, pulls up to the house across the street, the driver unaware of the trouble. The leather-jacketed toughs start to attack him as well, when Carrie's father rushes out, throws the toughs off the truck, and gets the driver away, all the time wielding a piece of pipe at the gang. He returns to his house, saying "niggers and white niggers," as if "that explained everything" (198).

A well-meaning attempt to suggest that some, perhaps most, of the parents involved in the controversy about busing children of one color to a school predominantly of another are people caught between opposing forces, this story in reality seems so equivocal as to be ineffectual. Though the children in the family would no doubt be able to handle the day in school, their elders have a far more deeply seated emotional commitment to the status quo. Carrie's father is a "good" man in that he hates what he sees as injustice no matter on whom the injustice is performed. Hence his defense of the black driver, though no doubt earning him the label of "nigger lover" from the gang of toughs, is consistent with his detesting those who forcibly try to change the existing social order. To him, "niggers and white niggers" are alike in that neither has any real interest in the issue at hand, the children's education, only in causing unrest and trouble. Just as his children, he feels, would be caught in the crossfire if they went to school that day, so the black driver too was innocently caught in the crossfire as he attempted merely to do his job. Very dated now, the story no doubt fit a particular frame of mind in the mid-1960s when it was first published, but it reveals little about the emotions of the central figures involved, only the reflexlike behavior of the older people in the community. As a story, it offers no challenge except to reveal the father's

ambiguous frame of mind in which he sees hoodlums and those supporting equal schooling as basically the same kind of human being.

O   *"The Lovely April"*

One of Grau's better characterizations of an eccentric is "Mr.
Robin," a little man coming in on the train as "The Lovely April"
opens. Evidently rather simpleminded and prone to unconventional
behavior (such as coming to church wearing a hat, under which his
head sports a pancake topped with a fried egg), but basically innocent,
harmless, and a victim rather than a victor, Mr. Robin lives comforta-
bly as a result of being from a well-to-do family. And this day, he
comes to live in a small town where he would be more protected than
he could be in the city. In time he parasitically attaches himself to the
family of the narrator, and he sits throughout the day talking to the
black cook, Oriole, in the narrator's home. Oriole, a powerful woman
who had rid herself of several husbands previously, comes to love Mr.
Robin, she misses him when he is not in her kitchen, and she wishes to
protect him at all times. When Mr. Robin's father writes to have him
returned to the city, Oriole sells her farm, packs up her belongings in
a wagon, and leaves to take Mr. Robin to the train. The train is barely
out of town before it has to stop because of a granite monument sitting
on the tracks. During the melee which follows, Mr. Robin walks out of
the train unnoticed, presumably taken by Oriole up to the high ridges
of the hills where they can live together.

This is an unusual story in at least one major respect: it is one of the
few examples in Grau's work where humor is deliberately introduced
and where it fits the subject matter. Akin to the frontier tall-tale, "The
Lovely April" is an ironic commentary on various forms of social intercourse, including the powerful woman saving the weak man, the "love
conquers all" concept in which even color differences are overlooked
by those involved, the "God's fool" idea of the simple man being in
some indefinable way closer to truth and virtue than those more cynical souls around him, and so on. The monument was presumably
placed on the tracks by Oriole, since she is more powerful than most
of the men mentioned in the story, and it would be only through this
means that she could "save" Mr. Robin. And the story takes on some
of the mythic quality so prominent in Grau's earlier collection of stories
and which is almost wholly absent from this one. It is an amusing story

and a serious story at the same time, and it is among the best pieces in this book.

P *"The Way Back"*

Two lovers are driving back to the state capital after spending some time together, and in the city she gets in her car while he drives away in his, each to his or her respective mate. "The Way Back" is a story about adultery, seen particularly from the perspective of the woman who knows that a part of her life is over but who is not sure how to describe what really happened in the relationship:

And what was left. Something back inside your head. Way back in your head, inside the shelter of the skull, hidden by the bone. Encircled by the gray cells, fed by the blood. But it wasn't anything at all. (223)

As she drives out of the city, his car follows, till she turns off in her direction while he continues back where they had come from. Holding an acorn, she reflects: "One life or another. And what came out of sex now. Love maybe. But what wasn't as sure as a tree. Or maybe a tree was as sure as love. One capsule life or another" (224). And as she drives to her own home, the "sounds and movements of her body kept her from remembering: that kind of loneliness was the next thing to death" (225).

The story is somewhat like Noël Coward's bittersweet *Brief Encounter* in that two married people have to end their affair; as they separate, they strain for one last glimpse of each other, with the love they share more valid than the one they are legally bound to share with their mates. But by now this idea has been worked to death, and Grau's version does not rise above the usual pattern. One may sympathize with the woman in particular, since the story is told from her point of view. And the isolation noticed earlier as predominant emotionally in this collection is even more obvious in this story than in the others.

But as a work of fiction, this simply does not have sufficient development for it to be as dramatically valid as one would desire. The reader, for example, knows nothing about the two people's mates, what drove the couple to each other, what they derived from each other, and, perhaps most importantly, why they are separating now, presumably for good. The story is an undeveloped anecdote, not a fully drawn tale of mature flesh-and-blood people. The comparison of human love with the acorn seems contrived and somewhat pretentious in that such a comparison is highly unlikely to occur when the woman's mind is primarily obsessed with her lover. As a whole, the story is a weak item in a collection of stories that ranges from excellent to embarrassing.

III   *Evaluation*

Just as Grau's career as a novelist has experienced its ups-and-downs, with some of her work decidedly inferior to others, so her short story output has varied widely. Her skills as a novelist, however, have shown genuine growth with her last two novels, but her more recent short stories are far from her best efforts. *The Black Prince and Other Stories* was a most distinguished debut for a writer of short stories, to a great extent, no doubt, because Grau knew her milieu and subject matter and was able to dig out the riches potential in such material.

As she has changed focus, however, her work has lost much of the deep interest in her own world and the people inhabiting that world. On the one hand, it seems valuable for her to move away from the provincialism of the Gulf Coast region so emphasized in her first books, and in the recent novels she has found the expanse in which she can develop character and theme. In her more recent short fiction, however, she seems unable to develop characters as much as seems necessary, nor to probe more vigorously into the subjects about which the characters are concerned. In some recent stories she seems to have taken the easy way out—not just those dealing with topical issues, but even more with those handling familiar subjects or variations on the one central issue of this collection, the isolation and solitude experienced by women, in particular, who find death or some other force out of their control altering their expected directions in life.

The Wind Shifting West would no doubt be a stronger collection if it had been limited more selectively to, say, another nine stories. Some of the tales in this collection are solid and well worth comparing with most of those in the earlier collection. Some are successful forays into new (for Grau) territory, such as the apocalyptic "The Last Gas Station." Yet such a large number of these stories are so embarrassingly weak that one wishes he could avoid discussing them at all, were it not necessary for the sake of completeness in treating her output of short fiction.

To say that her shorter work is a "mixed bag" would be to say the obvious, but it would not offer any answers to the questions of why her career as a writer of short fiction developed as it did, nor would it be possible here to offer such suggestions. One must note, however—and bemoan—the fact that, as rich a book as *The Black Prince and Other Stories* was, *The Wind Shifting West* was, to the same degree, a disappointing book.

Still, Grau remains an important figure in the history of the American short story, and indeed her lasting status as a writer may be more as a writer of the shorter form than of the novel. A number of her stories remain uncollected, and although the total output of such stories is not as great as that of, say, Flannery O'Connor, she fully warrants the claim that at her best, in terms simply of the quality of her best work if not in terms of quantity of production or consistent productivity, she ranks with O'Connor, Eudora Welty, and Carson McCullers.[7] Hence the failings found in her second collection of stories should not be construed to suggest that her overall career as a storywriter is in dispute, only that she remains as inconsistent in quality in the writing and publishing of the story as of the novel.

CHAPTER 8

A Regionalist Beyond Regionalism

THERE is no denying the fact that Grau's career has moved in several distinctly different directions since she began to write professionally. Like so many younger authors, she suffered from hyperbolic overpraise for her first published fiction. The critical commonplace that her early work is her best[1] remains true, and it is this early work that seems in retrospect to have prompted the most wildly inappropriate acclaim, as critics outdid each other in finding authors with whom to compare Grau. The praise she received for *The Black Prince and Other Stories* was little short of adulation, as when *Time* said that the collection was "the most impressive U.S. short story debut . . . since J. D. Salinger's *Nine Stories*."[2] In 1963 she was said to have the potential of Flannery O'Connor, William Styron, and Truman Capote.[3] Another critic compared the "circumstantial solidity" of her fiction to the realism of Balzac and Flaubert,[4] and another compared her stories to those written by Chekhov and Katherine Mansfield.[5] Added to these were the occasional comparisons to the work of William Faulkner, Carson McCullers, and Robert Penn Warren, and one can conclude quite easily that this collected (and premature) acclaim was simply too immense a load for a young writer to carry.

For with such enthusiastic praise as she received for her early books, there was simply no way for anyone short of a Faulkner to continue the pace. And Grau, though a writer with decidedly well-developed talent, is simply not so consistently in the same league as some of those with whom she has been compared. Consequently, when she changed subjects, techniques, or locales, the inevitable revisionist thinking set in, with critics trying to balance their earlier excessive praise with excessive reproach that was fully as hyperbolic.

A more balanced initial reception, in retrospect, would no doubt have been preferable to the acclaim, for it is undeniable that much of what Grau does is craftsmanlike, perceptive, and enduring, just as it is true that much is unconvincing, stereotyped, and curiously thin; what she does well she does very well indeed, but when she falters, the result can be embarrassing. Among the things she does best are handling regional characters, settings, and issues; probing into the manipulations of those seeking power, wealth, and influence; and depicting primitive, even primordial, forces in conflict. Among the things she seems to handle less well are creating urban (as opposed to rural) people involved in their humdrum daily pace, probing deeply into character motivation, and demonstrating any overriding philosophical perspective governing her fiction.

As a regional novelist, for example, Grau is particularly effective in delineating the manner in which her characters—particularly blacks and primitives—move easily through settings which in other hands would be merely picturesque or romantic. As one critic noted persuasively, "nature is her vision, the focal point of her best fiction,"[6] with "nature" in this case implying the pervasive sense of animal and plant references and imagery that in themselves constitute, for this critic, a "vision" of indifference and impartiality.[7] Indeed, Grau's objective handling of her characters' lives is often cited as one of her special strengths.[8] Her sense of "place" is strong, and Grau's best work is that growing out of her lifelong experience with the hot, humid Gulf Coast below New Orleans.

One can see, again in retrospect, that much of her fiction is concerned with various kinds of love and power, as well as with the manipulations of others that so often is a part of craving such love or power. Not surprisingly, most of her characters seem incapable of a mature acceptance of either of these two forces in life, for both readers and writers find accounts of depravity, evil, hatred, and power-hunger more persuasive as fictional subjects than the seemingly naive celebration of pure love, mature handling of power, and rejection of evil in one's life would be.

Grau's characters, even when caught up in the fervor of demanding love or power, seldom become as complex as one would desire; rarely, for example, do her characters take on the tragic nature so familiar to readers of Faulkner, O'Connor, or some other Southern writers. It almost seems as if Grau is sometimes willing to take the easy way out of her examination of the human dilemma by creating people who are potentially rich, because of their fascination with various forms of control over others, but who simply do not grow sufficiently in the reader's mind to be completely persuasive. All too often these characters simply exist, lacking any substance other than their lust or sense of duty or whatever. One is tempted to agree with those critics who have used the term "bloodless"[9] to refer to some of Grau's characters, were this term too insufficient to be perfectly valid. For at her best Grau can, through a few scenes or snatches of dialogue, give us a convincing portrayal of individuals who come completely alive for us. It is, rather, in those characters in whom we would expect more such solidity—such as the protagonist-narrators of *The Condor Passes* and *Evidence of Love*—who should reflect, from their vantage point of long and active lives, a much more complex vision of themselves, their motives, and their rise to positions of power. As it is, all too often such struggles as are recounted seem to be relatively simple matters of good versus evil, the "good guys" against the "bad guys," as with the conflicts between Abigail Mason Howland and her husband's world in *The Keepers of the House*.

On more formal grounds, one can see that Grau's strength is more as a stylist than as a constructor; that is, she is better at creating a sense of mystery or an atmosphere laden with exotic sensory stimuli than she is in creating plots that end conclusively. A good deal of her fiction simply ends, as with the protagonist's death, or in other ways equally unsatisfying; and all too often her characters simply fall into a fetal position at moments of crisis, evidently a hysterical reaction to the problem requiring resolution in their lives. Simply as a storyteller, Grau is excellent, even if these stories sometimes are offered at the expense of "message" or thesis. As has often been noted, Grau has observed that she has "no cause and no message,"[10] a candid but disarming admission. For even without writing heavily thesis-laden works, works that clearly are written primarily to support one conviction or other, she surely could have suggested a greater commitment in her characters' lives. As it is, though, we sometimes simply do not get "inside" her characters sufficiently to be able to say what it is that motivates them or that causes them to respond to others as they do. Objectivity, then, is fine up to a point, but the reader often wishes for more of a sense of engagement in the characters' actions and responses.

In this respect, one should note Grau's effective, objective use of violence; through a simple, usually direct style, her uncomplicated characters enter into violent situations as often because of circumstances as because of deeply flawed personalities. The term "documentary" has been used to discuss this aspect of Grau's work, to indicate her tendency to record rather than to interpret.[11] For since Grau works "without a dominant theme or an explicit philosophical view,"[12] even her use of violence is less an example of grotesquerie in her characters than it is their sole means of reacting against injustice, hatred, or whatever; it is simply their reaction against "anxiety, frustration, and insecurity."[13]

One cannot, then, claim that Grau is a novelist of the first rank, although at least three of her novels—*The Hard Blue Sky, The Keepers of the House,* and *Evidence of Love*—are in their respective ways excellent works that match anything similar produced in recent American fiction. One can say, though, that she is an important short story writer, for even though this aspect of her career is inconsistent, there are enough excellent tales, especially those in *The Black Prince and Other Stories,* to warrant their being reprinted, anthologized, and studied for many years to come. And even in those stories that seem less than memorable—because of insufficiently realized characters, plots, or conflicts—there is always a fine sense of mood, setting, description, and the sensuous possibilities of narrative.

Grau, therefore, is a fine example of the regional novelist whose best work surpasses mere regionalism, whose other work is always interesting even when deeply flawed, and whose overall career, despite the early extremes of praise accorded it, has been a steady, sure development of one who sees that the many forms of love, evil, and power possible in human life are best personified in the lives of ordinary people from the region she knows—and loves—the best. All in all, this is no small achievement, and one cannot omit the possibility that her future career as a writer will take even more changes of direction as she continues to explore the machinations of evil in human life.

Notes and References

Chapter One

1. Quoted by Roddy Paul, "Orleanian Gets Pulitzer Prize." *New Orleans Times-Picayune*, May 4, 1965; John Hohenberg, *The Pulitzer Prizes* (New York, Columbia University Press, 1974), p. 2.

2. Quoted in Don Lee Keith, "A Visit with Shirley Ann Grau," *Contempora*, 2, no. 2 (1972), 12, an interview incorporating (without acknowledgment) portions of Henry Davis, Jr., "Shirley Ann Grau—On Books, Families, Schools," *Dixie Magazine, New Orleans Time-Picayune*, December 4, 1966, pp. 40, 42. All direct quotations from Grau included in this book that are otherwise not attributed, and many of the biographical details in this chapter, are taken from two extensive tape-recorded interviews with Grau conducted by Paul Schlueter: one at Metairie, Louisiana, on December 15, 1969, and the other at Chilmark, Martha's Vineyard, Massachusetts, on August 13, 1971; references to these interviews will be cited as "Interview, 1969" and "Interview, 1971," respectively. A number of other interviews granted by Grau contain basically similar responses to biographical questions.

3. "Shirley Ann Grau," in *World Authors, 1950–1970*, ed. John Wakeman (New York, H. W. Wilson, 1975), p. 590.

4. Keith, p. 11.

5. Davis, p. 40.

6. Interview, 1969.

7. Ibid.

8. Ibid.

9. Ibid.

10. Keith, p. 12.

11. Davis, p. 40.

12. Interview, 1969.

13. Quoted in Rose Kahn, "N. O. [New Orleans] Prizewinner Enjoys 'Delicious Bedlam,'" *New Orleans States-Item*, May 4, 1965.

14. "Billboard," *Carnival*, 4 (December, 1951), 3; Grau's story appeared in *Carnival*, 4 (October, 1951), 10–14.

15. *Carnival*, 2 (October, 1949), 38–40.

16. Lise Lelong, "Short Story Wins Her Toe-Hold As Writer," *New Orleans Item*, November 29, 1953.

17. Keith, p. 12.

18. Thomas Griffin, "Bell Ringer," *New Orleans Item*, February 4, 1955.

19. Davis, p. 40.

20. Keith, p. 11.

21. *New York Times Magazine*, August 15, 1965, pp. 26–27, 29–30, 32, 34, 36, 39.

22. Thomas D. Young et al., *The Literature of the South*, rev. ed. (Glenview, Ill., Scott Foresman, 1968); John M. Bradbury, *Renaissance in the South* (Chapel Hill, University of North Carolina Press, 1963); Frederick J. Hoffman, *The Art of Southern Fiction* (Carbondale, Southern Illinois University Press, 1967); and other works cited in the bibliography.

23. Keith, p. 14.

24. Interview, 1969.

25. Mary Campbell, "Miss Grau Eyes Her Novel," *New Orleans Times-Picayune*, June 27, 1965 (an article subsequently distributed by the Associated Press and reprinted in numerous other American newspapers).

26. Ibid.

27. Cited both by Campbell and by Keith, p. 14.

28. Campbell.

29. *New Orleans Times-Picayune*, March 18, 1966.

30. Interview, 1969.

31. Keith, p. 11.

32. Ibid.

33. Ibid.

34. *New Orleans Times-Picayune*, July 11, 1964.

35. See Merrill Maguire Skaggs, *The Folk of Southern Fiction* (Athens, University of Georgia Press, 1972), p. 151, among others, for a careless confusion of the two terms, and Louise Y. Gossett, *Violence in Recent Southern Fiction* (Durham, N.C., Duke University Press, 1965), p. 194, among others, for a clear awareness of the distinctions between the terms.

36. All quotations from "The Essence of Writing," *The Writer*, May, 1974, pp. 14–15.

37. "Shirley Ann Grau," in Wakeman, p. 592.

38. All quotations from Ralph Daigh, "Answers from a Pulitzer Prize-Winning Housewife: Shirley Ann Grau," in *Maybe You Should Write a Book* (Englewood Cliffs, N.J., Prentice-Hall, 1977), p. 118.

39. Keith, p. 14.

40. Ibid.

41. Daigh, p. 120; ellipses in the original. Similar thoughts are found in Keith, p. 14.

42. Wakeman, p. 591.

43. Kahn.

Chapter Two

1. Interview, 1969.

2. *The Hard Blue Sky* (New York, Alfred A. Knopf, 1958); page references to this edition appear parenthetically in the text.

3. Interview, 1969.

4. Ibid.

5. Ibid.

6. Ibid.

7. Ann Pearson, "Shirley Ann Grau: Nature is the Vision," *Critique*, 17, no. 2 (1975–1976), 49.

8. Chester E. Eisinger, "Grau, Shirley Ann," in *Contemporary Novelists*, ed. James Vinson (New York, St. Martin's Press, 1972), p. 515.

9. Bradbury, p. 131.

Chapter Three

1. *The House on Coliseum Street* (New York, Alfred A. Knopf, 1961); page references to this edition appear parenthetically in the text.

2. Interview, 1969.

3. Ibid.

4. Jack DeBellis, "Two Southern Novels and a Diversion," *Sewanee Review*, 70 (October–December 1962), 691–92.

5. Alwyn Berland, "The Fiction of Shirley Ann Grau," *Critique*, 6, no. 1 (1963), 82.

6. Eisinger, p. 516.

Chapter Four

1. Quoted in "Shirley Ann Grau, N.O. Author, Pulitzer Winner," *New Orleans States-Item*, May 3, 1965.

2. Carlton Cremeens, "An Exclusive Tape Recorded Interview with Shirley Ann Grau," *Writer's Yearbook*, no. 37 (1966), 22.

3. Ibid.

4. William T. Going, "Alabama Geography in Shirley Ann Grau's *The Keepers of the House*," *Alabama Review*, 20, i (1967), 62–68.

5. Quoted in ibid., p. 68, n.

6. Campbell.

7. Quoted in "Tips," *Publishers' Weekly*, March 30, 1964, p. 41.

8. Cremeens, p. 22.

9. *The Keepers of the House* (New York, Alfred A. Knopf, 1964); page numbers for this edition appear parenthetically in the text.

10. Domingo Pérez Minik, "Shirley Ann Grau y los Atridas de Madison City," *Insula*, 21, Nos. 236–37 (July–August 1966), 27.

11. Campbell.

12. Pérez Minik, p. 237 (translated by Fred Alvarez).

13. Quoted in Going, p. 68, n.

14. Cremeens, p. 22.

15. Ibid.

Chapter Five

1. Interview, 1969.
2. Keith, p. 14.
3. *The Condor Passes* (New York, Alfred A. Knopf, 1971); page references to this edition appear parenthetically in the text.
4. Grau has commented that the novel's title refers to a Bolivian or Peruvian folksong, and that Simon and Garfunkel, in their popular version, "El Condor Pasa," managed "to absolutely corrupt" the original (Interview, 1971).
5. Denis Donaghue, "Life Sentence," *New York Review of Books,* December 2, 1971, p. 28; review of *The Condor Passes* and other novels published in late 1971.
6. Originally published as "The Condor Passes," *Atlantic,* 219 (January, 1967), 62–67, 71, 73; republished and retitled as "Stanley," in *The Wind Shifting West* (New York, Alfred A. Knopf, 1974), pp. 226–47.
7. Gay Talese, *Honor Thy Father* (Greenwich, Conn., Fawcett Books, 1971), p. 186.
8. Donaghue, p. 29.

Chapter Six

1. Don Lee Keith, "New Orleans Notes," *Delta Review,* no. 2 (1965), p. 12.
2. Jack Conroy, "Shirley Ann Grau and a Mess of Gumbo," *Panorama Magazine, Chicago Daily News,* September 11–12, 1971, p. 12.
3. R. Z. Sheppard, "Cold Comforts," *Time,* February 7, 1977, p. 90.
4. *Evidence of Love* (New York, Alfred A. Knopf, 1977); page references to this edition appear parenthetically in the text.
5. As quoted by Harry T. Moore in his definitive critical biography of D. H. Lawrence, *The Priest of Love,* 2d ed. (New York, Farrar, Straus and Giroux, 1974), p. vii.
6. *The Wind Shifting West* (New York, Alfred A. Knopf, 1973), pp. 55–69; this story was evidently not previously published separately in periodical form.

Chapter Seven

1. Interview, 1969.
2. *The Black Prince and Other Stories* (New York, Alfred A. Knopf, 1954); page references to this edition appear parenthetically in the text.
3. Michelle Murray, "Shirley Ann Grau: A Writer Whose Promise Was Not Fulfilled," *Washington Post,* November 27, 1973, p. B6.

4. Anatole Broyard, "Books of the Times: Quitting While She's Ahead," *New York Times*, November 1, 1973, p. 41.

5. *The Wind Shifting West* (New York, Alfred A. Knopf, 1973); page references to this edition appear parenthetically in the text. Grau's own comments about this story, the only one she has discussed in print, make basically the same points as I do; see "Notes on 'The Black Prince'" in *An Introduction to Literature* ed. Mary Rohrberger et al. (New York, Random House, 1968), pp. 320–21.

6. *The Reporter*, June 22, 1961, pp. 23–25.

7. Arthur Voss, *The American Short Story: A Critical Survey* (Norman, Okla., University of Oklahoma Press, 1975), p. 350.

Chapter Eight

1. See, e.g., Hoffman, p. 106.
2. January 24, 1955, p. 92.
3. Bradbury, p. 197.
4. Gossett, p. 179.
5. Carl VanVechten, quoted in Berland, p. 78.
6. Pearson, p. 48.
7. Ibid., p. 58.
8. Gossett, p. 179; Eisinger, p. 515.
9. Doris Grumbach, "Highly Charged Tale of Static Lives," *Los Angeles Times Book Review*, March 20, 1977, p. 8 (review of *Evidence of Love*); Van Allen Bradley, "Shirley Ann Grau's Latest, Bloodless and Loveless Novel," *Panorama Magazine, Chicago Daily News*, March 5, 1977 (review of *Evidence of Love*).
10. Earle F. Walbridge, "Shirley Ann Grau," *Wilson Library Bulletin*, 34 (1959), 250.
11. Gossett, p. 180.
12. Ibid., 193.
13. Ibid., 14.

Selected Bibliography

PRIMARY SOURCES

1. Collections of Short Stories
The Black Prince and Other Stories. New York: Knopf, 1954.
The Wind Shifting West. New York: Knopf, 1973.

2. Novels
The Condor Passes. New York: Knopf, 1971.
Evidence of Love. New York: Knopf, 1977.
The Hard Blue Sky. New York: Knopf, 1958.
The House on Coliseum Street. New York: Knopf, 1961.
The Keepers of the House. New York: Knopf, 1964.

3. Stories
"The Beach Party." *Redbook,* 125 (September, 1965), 54–55, 147–48, 155, 160: Reprinted in *The Wind Shifting West.*
"The Beginning of Summer." *Story,* 34 (November, 1961), 61–70.
"The Burglar." *Saturday Evening Post,* 241 (October 19, 1968), 68–71, 74. Retitled "The Householder" and reprinted in *The Wind Shifting West.*
"The Condor Passes." *Atlantic,* 219 (January, 1967), 62–67, 71, 73. Retitled "Stanley" and reprinted in *The Wind Shifting West.*
"Eight O'Clock One Morning." *Reporter,* 24 (June 22, 1961), 23–25. Reprinted in *The Wind Shifting West.*
"The Empty Night." *Atlantic,* 209 (May, 1962), 49–56.
"The First Day of School." *Saturday Evening Post,* 234 (September 30, 1961), 54–55, 58–60.
"The Fragile Age." *Carnival,* 4 (October, 1951), 10–14.
"Hunter's Home." *Mademoiselle,* 45 (September, 1957), 122–23, 172–79. Included, in slightly different form, in *The Hard Blue Sky,* pp. 262–74.
"Isle aux Chiens." In *New World Writing: Tenth Mentor Selection.* New York: New American Library, 1956. Pp. 176–95. Included, in slightly different form, in *The Hard Blue Sky,* pp. 54–75.
"Joshua." *New Yorker,* 30 (February 20, 1954), 30–40. Reprinted in *The Black Prince and Other Stories.*
"The Keepers of the House." *Ladies' Home Journal,* 31 (January–February, 1964), 92–94, 96, 98, 100, 102–4, 106–12, 114–27. Condensed version of *The Keepers of the House.*

"The Longest Day." *New Yorker*, 31 (September, 1955), 30–34. Retitled "The Long Afternoon" and reprinted in *The Wind Shifting West*.

"The Loveliest Day." *Saturday Evening Post*, 235 (May 5, 1962), 30–31, 68–69.

"The Lovely April." *Shenandoah*, 13 (Autumn, 1961), 3–18. Reprinted in *The Wind Shifting West*.

"The Man Below." *Atlantic*, 206 (September, 1960), 64–68. Retitled "The Thieves" and reprinted in *The Wind Shifting West*.

"One Night." *Gentleman's Quarterly*, 36 (February, 1966), 64–65, 102, 104, 106, 109–10.

"The Other Way." *Vogue*, 140 (August 15, 1962), 87, 134. Reprinted in *The Wind Shifting West*.

"Pillow of Stone." *Redbook*, 119 (August 1962), 32–33, 71–73. Reprinted in *The Wind Shifting West*.

"The Reach of the Fog." *Saturday Evening Post*, 235 (October 6, 1962), 68–72. Retitled "The Land and the Water" and reprinted in *The Wind Shifting West*.

"Sea Change." *Atlantic*, 220 (November, 1967), 105–9. Reprinted in *The Wind Shifting West*.

"The Sound of Silver." *New Mexico Quarterly*, 23 (Summer, 1953), 127–52. Revised, retitled "The Black Prince," and reprinted in *The Black Prince and Other Stories*.

"Storm." *New Yorker*, 31 (September 24, 1955), 41–48. Included, in slightly different form, in *The Hard Blue Sky*, pp. 446–56, 457–60, 462–64.

"Stranger at the Window." *Saturday Evening Post*, 232 (May 28, 1960), 30, 54, 56–57, 60. Retitled "The Man Outside" and reprinted in *The Wind Shifting West*.

"The Things You Keep." *Carnival*, 3 (December, 1950), 11–13.

"The Way Back." *Southern Review*, n.s. 3 (April, 1967), 407–15. Reprinted in *The Black Prince and Other Stories*.

"White Girl, Fine Girl." In *New World Writing: Fourth Mentor Selection*. New York: New American Library, 1953. Pp. 282–302. Reprinted in *The Black Prince and Other Stories*.

"Wind Shifting West." *Cosmopolitan*, 161 (August, 1966), 90–94, 128–29. Reprinted in *The Wind Shifting West*.

"The Young Men." *Redbook*, 130 (April, 1968), 64–65, 136–38.

4. Miscellaneous Nonfiction

"The Essence of Writing." *The Writer*, 87 (May, 1974), 14–15. Reprinted in *The Writer's Handbook, 1977*, ed. A. S. Burack, pp. 15–17. Boston: The Writer, 1977.

"The Felicitous Felicianas." *Venture*, 3 (August–September, 1966), 73–76.

Foreword. *Old Creole Days*, by George Washington Cable. New York: New American Library, 1961. Pp. vii–xiii.

"Galatoire's of New Orleans." *Holiday*, 20 (October, 1956), 64–67, 70–71, 73.

Introduction. *Cross Creek*, by Marjorie Kinnan Rawlings. New York: Time, 1966. Pp. xv–xxi.

"Mansions on the Mississippi." *Holiday*, 17 (March, 1955), 98–100, 134–35, 137, 139.

"Mississippi's Magic Coast." *Holiday*, 17 (June, 1955), 60–63, 145, 147, 149.

"New Orleans Society." *Holiday*, 23 (March, 1958), 82–87, 115, 118–21.

"Notes on 'The Black Prince.'" In *An Introduction to Literature*, ed. Mary Rohrberger et al. New York: Random House, 1968. Pp. 320–21.

"Perfumed City." *McCall's*, 95 (April, 1968), 112.

"Two Portraits of the Artist." *Carnival*, 2 (October, 1949), 38–40.

"The Vineyard Is the Place to Go." *New York Times Magazine*, August 15, 1965, pp. 26–27, 29–30, 32, 34, 36, 39.

5. Interviews

CAMPBELL, MARY. "Miss Grau Eyes Her Novel." *New Orleans Times Pica-yune*, June 27, 1965.

CREMEENS, CARLTON. "An Exclusive Tape-Recorded Interview with Shirley Ann Grau." *Writer's Yearbook*, no. 37 (1966), 20–22, 111–12.

DAIGH, RALPH. "Answers from a Pulitzer Prize-Winning Housewife: Shirley Ann Grau." In *Maybe You Should Write A Book*, ed. Ralph Daigh. Englewood Cliffs, N.J.: Prentice-Hall, 1977. Pp. 117–20.

DAVIS, HENRY, JR. "Shirley Ann Grau: Books, Families, Schools." *New Orleans Times-Picayune, Dixie Magazine*, December 4, 1966, pp. 40, 42.

DONOHUE, H. E. F. "Shirley Ann Grau." *Publishers Weekly*, 204 (December 3, 1973), 10, 13.

KAHN, ROSE. "N.O. Prizewinner Enjoys 'Delicious Bedlam.'" *New Orleans States-Item*, May 4, 1965.

KAY, JOAN. "With the Feiblemans, Two Writers are in Residence." *Louisville Courier Journal & News*, February 22, 1976. Reprinted in *Authors in the News*, ed. Barbara Nykoruk (Detroit: Gale Research Corp., 1976) II, 111.

KEITH, DON L. "New Orleans Notes." *Delta Review*, 2, no. 3 (1965), 11–12, 14.

———. "A Visit with Shirley Ann Grau." *Contempora*, 2, no. 2 (1972), 10–14.

ROHRBERGER, MARY. "Conversation with Shirley Ann Grau and James K. Fei-bleman." *Cimarron Review*, 43 (April, 1978), 35–45.

6. Bibliographies

GRAU, JOSPEH A. and Paul Schlueter. *Shirley Ann Grau: An Annotated Bib-liography*. New York, Garland, 1981.

GRISSOM, MARGARET S. "Shirley Ann Grau: A Checklist." *Bulletin of Bibliography*, 28 (July–September, 1971), 76–78.

SECONDARY SOURCES

BERLAND, ALWYN. "The Fiction of Shirley Ann Grau." *Critique*, 6, no. 1 (1963), 78–84. Praises Grau's technical skills but laments lack of emotional or intellectual commitment in her first three books.

BONIFAS, ANNE–MARIE. "Sur un Problème Sudiste: Shirley Ann Grau at les Fantomes du Passé." *Études Anglo-Américaines* (Annales de la Faculté des Lettres et Sciences Humaines de Nice, 27 [1976]). Paris: Belles Lettres, 1976, pp. 97–108. A general discussion (in French, with many bibliographic errors) of Grau's novels as they relate to traditional concepts of "Southern womanhood" and black-white relations; comparisons with works by Faulkner and Ralph Ellison are included.

BRADBURY, JOHN M. *Renaissance in the South: A Critical History of the Literature, 1920–1960*. Chapel Hill: University of North Carolina Press, 1963. P. 131. Brief discussion of Grau's first three books.

COLES, ROBERT. "Mood and Revelation in the South." *New Republic*, 150 (April 18, 1964), 17–19. Praises *The Keepers of the of the House* as accurate portrayal of prejudice.

DEBELLIS, JACK. "Two Southern Novels and A Diversion." *Sewanee Review*, 70 (October–December, 1962), 691–94. Hostile but perceptive, sees *The House on Coliseum Street* as featuring a "non-introspective protagonist confronted with cliches that substitute for real people."

DONAGHUE, DENIS. "Life Sentence." *New York Review of Books*, 17 (December 2, 1971), 28–30. Generally insightful review of *The Condor Passes*; notes Grau's detachment and control in moving narrative from character to character.

EISINGER, CHESTER E. "Grau, Shirley Ann." In *Contemporary Novelists*, ed. James Vinson. New York: St. Martin's Press, 1972, pp. 514–16. Though acknowledging Grau's "tough, cold, and realistic" work, dismisses her as a mere "local colorist" who lacks originality and a "complex vision."

GOING, WILLIAM T. "Alabama Geography in Shirley Ann Grau's *The Keepers of the House*." *Alabama Review*, 20, no. 1 (1967), 62–68. Valuable close reading of Grau's geographical references to show how carefully she structured the novel.

GOSSETT, LOUISE Y. *Violence in Recent Southern Fiction*. Durham, N.C.: Duke University Press, 1965. Excellent discussion of Grau's objective, "straightforward" style, but criticizes her tendency to "oversimplify human relationships"; violence seen as a function of her characters' primitive natures.

"Grau, Shirley Ann." In *World Authors, 1950–1970*, ed. John Wakeman.

New York: H. W. Wilson, 1975, pp. 590–92. Brief biographical piece, including an autobiographical note by Grau.

"The Hard Blue Sky." in *Survey of Contemporary Literature*, ed. Frank N. Magill. Rev. ed. Englewood Cliffs, N.J.: Salem Press, 1977. VI, 3253–56. Notes Grau's emphasis on place, her sense of style, and her avoiding a recreation of "the regional scene in Faulknerian terms."

HOFFMAN, FREDERICK J. *The Art of Southern Fiction: A Study of Some Modern Novelists*. Carbondale: Southern Illinois University Press, 1967. Pp. 106–9. Discusses all of Grau's novels, but emphasizes *The Keepers of the House*, noting that despite a number of virtues in the book, she is not "the master strategist of Southern history."

HOHENBERG, JOHN. *The Pulitzer Prizes*. New York: Columbia University Press, 1974. Pp. 2, 255–56. Brief discussion of Grau's reception of the Pulitzer Prize.

HUSBAND, JOHN D. *New Mexico Quarterly*, 28 (Spring, 1958), 61–65. Grau's creative-writing professor discusses *The Hard Blue Sky*'s qualities of design and construction and her mastery of the novelist's craft.

JOHNSON, RICHARD A. "The Keepers of the House." In *Survey of Contemporary Literature*, ed. Frank N. Magill. Rev. ed., vol. 7. Englewood Cliffs, N.J.: Salem Press, 1977, pp. 3981–83. Notes Grau's emphasis on encounter between man and a hostile natural world and the characters' need to remain faithful to the "archetypal frontier experience."

KEITH, DON L. "Shirley Ann Grau: Chasing the Creative Muse Through the Land of the Lotus Eaters." *Louisiana Renaissance*, 1 (October, 1977), 18–19, 44. Based greatly on Keith's 1972 interview with Grau; small amount of new material of slight interest.

LUEDTKE, LUTHER S. "The Condor Passes." In *Survey of Contemporary Literature*, ed. Frank N. Magill. Rev. ed., vol. 3. Englewood Cliffs, N.J.: Salem Press, 1977, pp. 1513–16. Notes novel's suspenseful and intriguing qualities, as well as its forced symbolism and unclear focus.

MEEKER, RICHARD K. "The Youngest Generation of Southern Fiction Writers." In *Southern Writers: Appraisals in Our Time*, ed. R. C. Simonini, Jr., p. 186. Charlottesville: University Press of Virginia, 1964. Brief passage refers to Grau as "a regionalist who has not succumbed to provincialism."

PEARSON, ANN. "Shirley Ann Grau: Nature is the Vision." *Critique*, 17, no. 2 (December, 1975), 47–58. The role of nature in Grau's fiction is her "focal point," but it is sometimes presented so objectively that it "becomes meaningless, and, in turn, so does much of her fiction."

PÉREZ MINIK, DOMINGO. "Shirley Ann Grau y los Atridas de Madison City." *Insula*, 21, nos. 236–237 (1966), 27. A discussion (in Spanish) of the way Grau's protagonist in *The Keepers of the House* outmaneuvers the power-structure. Grau, compared to McCullers and McCarthy, does not write a social novel such as those by Steinbeck, but instead "places herself in a world of evocation."

ROHRBERGER, MARY. "'So Distinct a Shade': Shirley Ann Grau's *Evidence of Love.*" *Southern Review*, 14 (January, 1978), 195–98. Excellent analysis; meaning of novel based as much on silences and gaps in the narrative as on the voices and the story. The search for love in the novel turns out to be a "quest for order and understanding that can only come through an apprehension of shadows . . . , as reflected and reflecting images."

ROSE, ALAN HENRY. *Demonic Vision: Racial Fantasy and Southern Fiction.* Hamden, Conn.: Archon Books, 1976. Pp. 127–28. Brief discussion of "The Black Prince" as an example of the story of the demonic Negro, but notes differences from other examples.

ROSS, JEAN W. "Shirley Ann Grau." *Dictionary of Literary Biography, II: American Novelists Since World War II*, ed. Jeffrey Helterman and Richard Layman. Detroit: Gale Research Corp., 1978, pp. 208–215. General consideration of all of Grau's novels and of her major themes; notes that in her best work, "story and character were focused on a bond with the land," and that although she continues to experiment with multiple points of view and resists being categorized as a Southern writer, her later work suffers by "losing touch" with the Southern settings and characters which are her strengths.

TRACHTMAN, PAUL. "Rotten Roots." *The Progressive*, 28 (July, 1964), 41–43. Praises *The Keepers of the House* as a fable about "the context of Southern distress," but notes that Grau is neither a propagandist nor a moralist.

VOSS, ARTHUR. *The American Short Story: A Critical Survey.* Norman: University of Oklahoma Press, 1973. P. 352. Praises Grau's short fiction and ranks her with Welty, McCullers, and O'Connor.

WATKINS, FLOYD C. *The Death of Art: Black and White in the Recent Southern Novel.* Mercer University Lamar Memorial Lectures, no. 13. Athens: University of Georgia Press, 1970. Pp. 14, 20. After noting that "most southern novels which treat the relationship between the black man and the white man are highly prejudiced against the white," Watkins comments that "the marriage between the white Will Howland and the Negro Margaret [in *The Keepers of the House*] . . . is the most perfect perhaps in any modern fiction."

WILLIAMS, THOMAS. "Ducks, Ships, Custard, and a King." *Kenyon Review*, 24 (Winter, 1962), 184–88. Sees chief problem with *The House on Coliseum Street* as making the protagonist's "dullness" come alive for the reader and the effects this handicap has on style.

Index